WE THE PEOPLE

EVERYTHING FOLLOWS
THESE THREE WORDS

MARK A BUZZOTTA

ISBN 978-1-09838-140-0
ISBN eBook 978-1-09838-141-7

Special thanks to my wife who has endured my discussions and endless reviews of my written material. Leslie, if not for you, there wouldn't be a me.

This book is dedicated to my Chloe and Ariel who were the original inspirations for this book and much of my life. I hope this book means something to you.

This book is also dedicated to Colin and Lyndsey who have prompted me to think and re-think my positions, leading to an integrated, progressive and practical balance of innovative ideas. I hope this book will do the same for you

Special thanks to Michael Buzzotta, my brother, who is one of my inspirations and my best friend.

For more information, please go to
www.MarkABuzzotta.com

FOREWORD

Our Founding Parents did not birth this country for Republicans or Democrats, not for lobbyists or corporations, not for the wealthy or the powerful. Our Founding Parents built this country for WE THE PEOPLE.

This book is about what our Founding Parents intended when building our Democratic Republic which has become the most prosperous, most innovative, most scientifically and technologically advanced organization known to Humankind.

Our Founding Parents did not envision pure democracy, where the people control every aspect of government; nor did they envision a pure republic, where a representative or representatives of the people control every aspect of government. They designed a unique system where representatives would fulfill the will of the people while balancing the interests of the nation under the rule of written law.

The unique hallmark of our nation is our foundation upon Human Rights. Our nation was built on the concept that we are free to think for ourselves, express ourselves, worship as we will, and protect ourselves and our families. Consequently we are susceptible to all forces that neglect respect for the individual and employ power and strength to dominate and control. Just as the more sensitive child is vulnerable to the bully in the schoolyard, our nation is vulnerable to foreign powers that seek to dominate the U.S. and confiscate our resources. Centralized, command economies cannot survive without control over the free market or over free expression, and must dominate them to in order to perpetuate their system.

We the People are also experiencing an insidious erosion of our Constitutional freedoms from a variety of corporate, ideological, political and financial powers that seek dominion over our lives under the façade of creating a better way for all.

This book is about our nation's successes and failures as measured against the charge of our Founding Documents. If we follow the command of our Founding Parents, the possibilities for our future are astounding. More of our citizens will develop fantastic wealth; medical, scientific and technological advances will be unimaginable; and healthy life spans are likely to continue to extend. If we fail to follow more closely the direction of our Founding Parents as written in our Constitution, we risk losing everything we developed in the last 244 years including our prosperity, our freedoms, and all the advances that have led to the lifestyle we enjoy today, as the entire free world loses its largest and most loyal benefactor.

The issues discussed in this book transcend our social consciousness. Those in power seldom, if ever, mention the matters explored here. We are at a critical crossroad in this day and time. The concepts elucidated in this book will clearly describe each direction. The differences are stark and the correct direction is perfectly clear. Having the courage to take the proper road is the challenge incumbent upon you and me.

We the People….

EVERYTHING follows from these three words.

Everything in our Constitution,

Everything in our history as a nation, and

Everything in this book.

You are about to read THE MOST IMPORTANT MESSAGE of our time.

Table of Contents

INTRODUCTION

As "We the People" of the United States of America are the beneficiaries of the glorious country in which we are fortunate to live, we are also responsible for the faults and misdeeds of this nation.

More importantly, as a US citizen, I feel complicit in our faults. Therefore, I feel compelled to identify the problems, offer solutions, and attempt to correct our mistakes, so that we may move forward in a manner that is good for the people, the government, and the world, as we aspire to realize the ideals presented by our Founding Parents and the US Constitution.

Oftentimes in history, we come to a crossroad where we must make choices that are difficult but necessary. We are at that point in many areas in this country and in the world. We are at critical, pivotal junctures which require change to alter the course of history.

I will try to elucidate the problems and offer solutions in the following pages.

Hopefully these ideas will be accepted by the people and the powers that be, and we enact reforms that will benefit all the people for centuries, even millennia to come. The ideas here may offer a fresh perspective or may change your entire world view. In any case, I hope they make an impact.

I am not a Ph.D. in any field. I am not a politician or a bureaucrat with a lifetime of political experience. I am not a "one-percenter." I do not represent any party or group or organization, other than being a citizen of the

United States of America. I am not beholden to anyone or any organization. My commonness is my strength. I am just a person who was born in and has lived in the United States of American for over sixty years.

In order to present my case, I must first establish, as best I can, a description of who WE are and a brief history of the world and the U.S.A. After establishing my premise, I can build a case of where we are going. I will describe directions we are likely to follow if we do not accept my premise, and where we will go if we do. The differences are stark. Understanding the differences is critical for our survival.

I believe this effort is a work in progress and that all people need to contribute to creating a more perfect way. Therefore, I ask that you write me with your thoughts and suggestions. Though your contact information will not be published, sold or in any way released to any other person or organization, please understand that your comments and suggestions may be used in future writings, so if you do not want your comments reproduced, please indicate so. But please do write me at LetsMakeStraightOurWay@gmail.com.

CHAPTER I.

Back to the Beginning

We are now at violent odds with each other to the point that conflict has threatened apocalyptic catastrophe. Heated conflicts are prevalent between nations, cultures, races, religions, political parties, ideologies, communities, families, and the sexes. Each group has escalated its position and has been able to harness resources to develop their stature and fight their battles with ferocity. The result is violent clashes in all corners of the world.

The educated clash with the faithful; Democrats with Republicans; democratic countries with socialist/communist/centralized governments; religious extremists with moderates; unions with management; players with owners; liberals with conservatives; the Green Party with the high tech and the industrialists; women and men; Blacks and Whites; etcetera, etcetera, etcetera!

Respect, conflict resolution, tolerance and compromise have faded into the past with no vision of harmony on the distant horizon. And this trouble will not subside till we develop a new perspective.

I think we need to reconsider our commonalities and perspectives. We need to go back to basics. We need to look at everything with a fresh perspective. Therefore I am not writing as a Democrat or Republican, a liberal or conservative, a religious or secular individual, or an academic or religious person. If there is any description of my perspective, it is as an American, a citizen of the United States of America.

Everything that follows in this book follows from the first three words of our Constitution: We the People. And as everything in our nation's history has followed those three words, every point discussed in this book follows these three foundational words.

I write this book to serve two purposes: first to revisit our foundational values; and second to expose the interests that have perverted our values.

I wonder sometimes if our fundamental values have eroded or if they were never learned, as it seems contrary values are often taught to our children. Re-establishing these basic values is essential for us to resolve the problems we face together in the U.S. as well as the entire world.

First some very basic tenets:

We know that our earth is an anomaly in the known universe.

Despite our most highly developed technology, we have not found one other place in the universe that is like our earth. We have found no place that has the water, the atmosphere, similar gravitation, temperate climate, and a complex ecology like our earth. Scientists theorize given the enormity of our galaxy and the universe, that there may be other planets similar to ours, but there is no evidence, thus far.

NASA estimates there are 100 billion stars in our galaxy and there are 100 billion galaxies observable now, with more soon to follow. They say maybe 80% of the stars have planets, and a fraction of those are in zones where the distance from their star might have a temperature and potential climate that may allow life.

Then the planet must exist in a solar system that resembles ours so that it may be protected by outer larger planets, have a moon to stabilize its axial tilt and climate, have a relatively similar mass, size and metal core with similar gravitational properties, a thin crust, a similar size sun, a circular orbit rather than an elliptical orbit and a similar rotational velocity. (John Gribbon, *Alone in the Universe*)

Our earth is rare and needs to be appreciated.

Second, we know that there are many forms of life on this planet and that humankind is the highest, most complex form of life in the known universe. Scientists say the earth is about 4.5 billion years old and it took about a billion years for the simplest life to occur (www.space.com, "How Old Is Earth"). About 6 million years ago the earliest hominines appeared. (https://www.newscientist.com/article/dn17453-timeline-the-evolution-of-life/)

Human life is an exclusive and remarkable phenomenon that took over 4 billion years to develop, and whether it developed through the process of a fortunate set of random events or through the eminence of a Creator, Humankind is the pinnacle of life in the known universe.

Human life is extraordinarily rare and needs to be appreciated.

Third, we know that the civilized world on all continents up through the 1500s was organized by kingdoms of sorts where a king or ruling family held all the power and wealth and the people were merely subjects, chattel, or slaves of the rulers. History moved from the conquering of one people over another with the men and children taken as slaves of the victors and the women raped to eradicate the ethnicity. Living conditions were harsh. Lifespans were short. Disease was rampant. And life for centuries all over the world was abysmal.

We know that life changed in the 1600s when the Bible was widely distributed and people began to read. People began to realize that they were more than just property of a king, but rather children of a loving God.

We know that about 200 years later, a few men and women came along with new ideas and said that WE THE PEOPLE can manage ourselves. We don't need or want the king to do so for us. The United States was born of the idea that human beings are imbued with inalienable rights bestowed upon them by God; that people are children of God who have the right to think for themselves, speak their mind, worship God directly, and protect themselves and their families. The Great American Experiment was born.

These revolutionary concepts could not be quelled by any power. Not by the English Army. Not by the Japanese Empire and not by Nazi Germany. Thus greater advancements in science, medicine, longevity, technology, and lifestyle occurred in 244 years than in all of history over the entire planet.

The advancements occurred not only in America as a result of the creation of a Democratic Republic in the United States, but also around the world as democratic values spread everywhere. Extraordinary change occurred on the planet in a fraction of all civilized time. And it's because of humankind's newfound understanding of itself as described in Holy Scripture. Nothing can compare in any place or in any time.

Movements in the late Nineteenth Century and throughout the Twentieth Century developed in reaction to the free enterprise system in the United States with noble attempts to resolve issues related to poverty, crime, and corruption. Socialist and Communist systems developed through revolution in the Soviet Union and the Peoples Republic of China, as well as in Cuba, Nicaragua, Venezuela, and in Europe. Each one followed the paradigm proposed by Marx and Engels which suggested a better alternative to capitalism, while neglecting and even eliminating the rights of the individual. Centralized control became essential to direct each country's economy and to require their citizens' conformity to the values of the State. Consequently, despotism, not much different from Fascism, developed in these countries.

Lenin and Stalin felt that their country would not last if it did not match the industrial and financial success of the U.S. and the Allies, and they demanded that their people endure cruel labor conditions in a futile attempt to match the West. China's demand for conformity has eliminated creativity in its people, thus necessitating that they confiscate the innovation of the free nations. Essentially, the socialists and communists maintain a view that is void of the intrinsic value and intelligence of the individual. These governments believe that people do not have the inherent qualities to problem-solve, grow and excel on their own. They do not see Humankind as a marvelous being unique in the universe with intelligence incorporated into its being. Essentially they view their masses as no more than dependent, simplistic beings that must be controlled, directed and cared for by a more enlightened elite.

Christ, as noted in the Bible, was bold enough to suggest otherwise. And because of His revolutionary thought, the creative power of each individual under a free system was unleashed and now we live life more abundantly.

Whether one views the individual as a highly evolved member of the animal kingdom or a being imbued with the Spirit of God, all people can agree that Humankind is a remarkable creation that has proven to be capable of extraordinary accomplishment when free to utilize their own resources. No longer do we need to debate whether Science or Faith is true or flawed, as history suggests a confluence. No longer do we need to clash over political ideologies, as each has proven successes in certain areas and failures in others. No longer can extremist organizations, any culture, race, group, or sex claim superiority since no group can claim perfect self-sufficiency as opponents actually serve to define each group and are necessary for its long-term interests.

Leaders that cause divisions, for whatever reason, are limited in their vision and perspective. Ultimately, we all need the other side to survive. The great leaders in history have always been able to see an elevated, long-range perspective and lead the behavior of the masses toward the appreciation of the benefits of opposing sides. In other words, mutual respect is essential in conflict resolution.

As soon as people and their positions are reduced to labels, they become fractions of their whole being, and conflict inevitably occurs. And when these fractional positions are institutionalized, they perpetuate.

Conflicts nevertheless are inevitable. However, conflicts are actually the opportunity to expand one's view of oneself and the group, rather than battle over differences. Of course, this type of reasonableness is difficult when emotions cloud perspective.

Marx's concept of Dialectical Progress touches upon the method of movement in the universe and in social organizations, but it is rather limited and inaccurate.

Marx saw social movement as a "discussion" of sorts where ideas would swing from one idea to another opposing idea, sort of like a pendulum, however, in an upward or progressive manner. He suggested that all concepts and consequent social movements occurred in this fashion. He wrote that feudalism is eradicated by capitalism and then capitalism extinguished by socialism and then socialism would be transformed into communism. However, he missed a holistic view of this paradigm.

Let me use an example of light or radio or water waves. From the side view, the wave appears as an undulating two-dimensional structure of hills and valleys. The wave positioned upright or vertical rather than horizontal is the two-dimensional viewpoint of Marx as the development of thoughts swing back and forth on the undulating wave as it moves upward.

A three-dimensional view of a wave shows that the wave is not undulating, but rather moving in a spiral. From the side, a spiral appears as though it's an undulating wave, but that viewpoint is two-dimensional. Waves actually move in a three-dimensional spiral. Our planet and solar system move in the same fashion through our galaxy (https://www.youtube.com/watch?v=IJhg-ZBn-LHg). And the shape of the greatest piece of information created in the universe, DNA, is structured in the same spiral formation.

Marx's theories are flawed in that they are two-dimensional in a more complex world. If one looks at concepts from a two-dimensional view, it looks like concepts are exclusive and opposing, swinging from one opposing point to another, which is Marx's perspective. However, when one sees the history of an idea as it develops, one sees the connection of the ideas as interconnected, fluid concepts that are part of a greater whole.

Not only does the physical universe move in a spiral fashion, but concepts, self-consciousness, and social consciousness move in similar three- and four-dimensional manners...not in a two-dimensional manner as Marx suggested. Opposing concepts do not merely swing from one extreme to another, revolting against, nullifying and cancelling the later, but rather as three-dimensional concepts that have depth and four-dimensional concepts that have a past and a future. This wider view offers a new paradigm based on integration of historical data, prevailing views, and new possibilities. Progression of thought is rather like a circular staircase with ideas acting like steps moving in an upward spiral. Therefore, conflict is an opportunity and it is the substance that presents ideas for development and for social evolution. It takes leaders who understand these concepts and comprehend integrated development to help the masses through the disjointedness of conflict.

We know when we are left to our own resources, we excel, and excel marvelously as the last 244 years of US history has shown. It is only within the context of a free society where such social development can take place. When the individual is restricted from full expression of him/herself, then problem-solving, innovation, growth and progress is limited.

The remainder of this book will discuss the current issues being debated in our age and it will propose direction based upon the principles that We the People have the inherent ability and desire to manage ourselves.

CHAPTER II.

Problems in Our System

The Founding Parents of the United States of America laid the foundation for a free society where the will of the people would manage themselves within a free enterprise system. Implicit in this system is a respect for a collective intelligence among all the people. That is, if the people maintain a respect for the decisions of each individual within the whole, the whole will arrive at a point where the whole conceptualizes its direction together. However, once this system breaks down, progress is slowed or stopped.

The system can break down first by means of loss of respect for the individual and the groups that individuals created; that is, forgetting the preciousness of each individual as rare, intelligent and exclusive beings in the universe that are far more complex and intelligent than any label could encompass, regardless of whether the label is complimentary or disparaging. For example labeling one a "Yale graduate", or "Republican", or "Latino", or "male" or any classification fractionalizes the person and is the beginning of a loss of respect for the individual as a whole human being.

While a person is not limited to the label given him/her or to a group that she or he associates with, groups each have beneficial characteristics. Ignoring the beneficial attributes of a person's or a group's perspective neglects the value the participant finds in the group. However, seeking to understand the value offers the possibility of growth toward a greater whole. As each individual is endowed with an extraordinary intelligence, we must endeavor to understand and appreciate the perspective of each individual as an essential part of our whole consciousness. Understanding the benefits that a person or a group espouses is important for the upward spiral of progress.

The third manner in which progress is impeded is when others make decisions for the individual. This loss of autonomy happens when centralization occurs. Such limitations of growth and positive change are evident in socialized countries where despots harness the power and wealth and then regulate the masses in a system where the ruling party dictates. Centralizing the economy so that the manufacturing, pricing, and supply of all products and services are determined by a ruling body simply does not work as efficiently as market forces. The Soviet Union collapsed as a result. Communist China has to resort to imitation and illegal confiscation of ideas from the unsuspecting U.S. and the free world. Together, communist countries are responsible for at least 60 million deaths and more likely closer to 110 million deaths of their OWN people (David Satter "100 Years of Communism - and 100 Million Dead"; R.J. Rummel, *Murder by Communist Regimes*; Wikipedia, "Mass Killings by Communist Regimes"; Encyclopedia.com, "Communism, Population Aspects Of"). The mass genocide in each country terrified their masses into submitting to their ruling parties who gave their people no human rights whatsoever and treated them as mechanized, soulless entities. Unfortunately, an entire century of experimentation based on the flawed writings of Marx destroyed the lives of nearly one third to one half of the world's population through death and oppression in an attempt to eradicate the old dialectic of capitalism and Human Rights while posing an existential threat to life on our planet. (https://photius.com/rankings/world2050_rank.html, Total Population by Country)

Removing the decision-making process from the individual, whether by means of cultural discord or political structure, is extremely harmful to the survival of its people, and to other countries.

CHAPTER III.

These Four Problems
Can Ruin Us

We have four problems that are so massive that any one of them could literally ruin the United States.

1. We Have a National Debt of Over $25 Trillion.

It is seldom discussed by politicians regardless of the party. Occasionally, one might hear some comments from a politician, but it's usually brought up when one party doesn't want to support the ideas of another party. There has never been a concerted effort by anyone to correct the problem.

So what does $25 trillion in debt mean?

One reference point is from the banking industry. A bank will lend a borrower no more than three times their annual income. In other words, if a person wants to borrow money to purchase a house, the lending institution will ask the borrower to disclose his/her income records to determine what amount the borrower will qualify for, and then the bank will lend up to three times his/her annual income. So for example, the lending institution will lend $300,000 if the borrower has at least $100,000 in annual income.

At present, the U.S. has an annual income of $3.5 trillion a year from income tax and other various sources. (www.cbo.gov Monthly Budget Review: Summary for Fiscal Year 2019). This amount is a recent increase; it has been approximately half this amount only a few years ago. Nevertheless, at present, the U.S. should be able to borrow no more than $10.5 trillion by normal banking standards. US lawmakers have overspent the income of the U.S., which by the way is THE LARGEST INCOME OF ANY ORGANI-ZATION IN HISTORY, to the point that the U.S. has borrowed more than twice that amount!

I must balance my budget and my checkbook every month, but the US government doesn't! There is no institution that oversees the politicians and their out-of-control spending, except the people. So I ask, "Why hasn't anyone done anything?!"

Another reference point which personalizes the impact of the National Debt is the following example. In the mid-1990s, President Clinton and Speaker Gingrich, in an attempt to balance the US budget, instituted a tax that averaged $1000 per family in the United States. I was really upset with the increase as was everyone that I spoke with at that time. However, after a few days of thinking about the issue, I figured that if each family paying $1000 per year on average would make our country stronger and more stable, then I was sure I could manage $20 per week for such a cause. So, I relented, and suggested the same in my discussions with my friends and acquaintances.

Well, if for some reason, Congress and the U.S. instituted a $1000-per-family increase in taxes today that would be dedicated to paying off the National Debt, I would venture to say that there would be widespread and strong reaction against such an increase from every sector of our country. At least on the surface, an extra $1000 in taxes paid to the US government would seem to be an unjust and extraordinary burden for the average family.

There are approximately 100 million families in the U.S. Multiply 100,000,000 by $1000 and the result is $100 billion. That means that it would take 250 years for us to pay $25 trillion, that is, if there is NO MORE DEBT ADDED over the next 250 years. And that calculation doesn't even include interest! It will take more than 250 years to pay the $25 trillion dollar debt at the rate of an additional $1000 per year per family!

Here's another example of how this burdensome National Debt affects each one of us: If you take $25 trillion and divide it by every citizen in the U.S. (which is currently approximately 300 million people), then each citizen -- man, woman and child -- is currently responsible for paying $83,000 in ADDITIONAL taxes. What do you think of that fact?! That means that your children's future is burdened with a massive debt BEFORE THEY BEGIN WORKING! That means that each new child that is born a citizen of the United States comes into this world with a slap, not on their butt, but a slap on their face! WHAT A HORRIBLE THING WE HAVE DONE! We have overspent to the point that we have gorged ourselves at the expense of our children, and our children's children. And again I ask "Why hasn't anyone done anything?!"

There are about thirty-two million companies in the U.S. About twenty-five million are sole proprietors or independent contractors. (Albany Business Review, "What counts as a 'business'? April 11, 2019) Many say that since companies have more money than the people, then the companies should pay more money to solve this crisis. However, placing any of the burden on the companies only causes an increase in their prices for their products and services. Placing the burden on the companies in the U.S. is not helpful whatsoever, as the burden is ultimately on the American people.

Between the year 1776 and 2000 we overspent approximately $2 trillion as a nation cumulatively. Then from 2000 to 2020, we added over $23 trillion more to the National Debt. What does that fact say about our politicians over the last eighteen years! I believe what it says is that they have betrayed us, the citizens of the U.S., and have by any and every standard destroyed the financial stability of our country!

I have heard every contrary opinion regarding the National Debt from Nobel Prize-winning economists to politicians and pundits. The FACT of the matter is that YOU and I owe a massive amount to the US government that will burden us for a longer period in the future than the 244 years our Democratic Republic has been in existence! So, all those that diminish the extraordinary burden of this massive debt must have some ulterior motive for doing so.

2. We have career politicians that serve their own interests and the interests of lobbyists over the interests of the people that elected them.

Often, people enter politics with a concerted interest to represent their constituents with a fiduciary responsibility. However, with election cycles every few years (two to six), politicians quickly realize that the only way to become elected and reelected is to pander to their constituents and lobbyists. More often than not, the politician that becomes elected is the one that promises to bring home the bacon; that is, to get as much a portion of local, state, and federal dollars invested in their communities as possible. The politicians that are most successful at accomplishing this effort are the ones that are most likely to be elected and reelected. It's not a mystery. It is simply a fact of politics in the United States of America. Therefore, any fiduciary intent of politicians that may initially exist is quickly usurped by the need to be elected and reelected.

Additionally, the system allows factions or interest groups to lobby politicians with lavish gifts, money, and benefits through specific legal channels. Such a practice is no more than a legalized form of bribery. Lobbyists provide billions of dollars through campaign fundraising which gives the politicians a rather nice lifestyle as they hop from one campaign to the next while making the lawmaker indebted to the behind-the-scenes interest group. Also, lobbyists are allowed to make contributions to politicians' "non-profit organizations" or other companies tied to the lawmakers and to lawmakers' families. The groups that provide the largest and best gifts inevitably get the attention and favor of the political decision-makers, while We the People lose our power in government. Our elected officials now receive far more money from lobbyists and foreign interests than their government salaries, thereby redirecting their loyalty away from We the People.

It's certainly not a mystery why we have such a large Budget Deficit and National Debt. The system, as it is, actually encourages, incentivizes and perpetuates debt. And lobbying creates financial incentives that make the lawmakers rigidly stuck to their special interest supporters causing gridlock in government. Government of the people, by the people and for the people no longer exists.

So again I ask, "Why hasn't anyone done something?!"

3. **We live under the threat posed by centralized tyrannical governments which seek to control all the people and the economies of the entire world.**

The United States of America is called "The Great Experiment" because it is the only nation where Human Rights are the founding principle. Consequently, we are a target of other nations that see us as a vulnerable opportunity.

We had to defend ourselves from King George III and the United Kingdom of Great Britain in the 1700s.

We had to defend ourselves from the onslaught of the Japanese Empire and Nazi Germany in World War II.

We have to defend ourselves from the attacks of religious terrorists who believe their religious leaders should control our lives.

We have to defend ourselves from centralized governments like China and Russia who believe that they must control the economies of the world as well as all of the world's people.

Unlike economies that are built on Human Rights and Free Enterprise, socialist and communist countries cannot survive without being able to manipulate prices and production around the world. Therefore, it is an existential necessity that they seek to overthrow economies dependent on free enterprise. The fundamental problem is that command economies exist only if they can subjugate their people to perform as their State requires: the people are stripped of their inherent rights to freely think and express themselves, worship as they will and protect themselves; they are not allowed to problem-solve, excel or improve their own lives. Their people are subjugated to the values of their State. The paradigm of the socialists/communist/centralized countries is built on a faulty foundation and contrary to our appreciation of the marvel of life and our consequent value of Human Rights.

Russia is using the web to sow discord in our media and our institutions. They endeavor to corrupt our elections, steal our data and destroy our electronic infrastructure, while encroaching upon bordering democratic countries.

China is paying our universities extraordinary sums of money to "do research" on their behalf, while having their students learn advanced science and technology that is brought back to their country and potentially used against us. They are paying university professors extraordinarily large sums of money to recruit scientists to work for China and interests counter to the U.S. (US Department of Justice, "Harvard University Professor and Two Chinese Nationalist Charged in Three Separate China Related Cases") They require that any company that does business in China have placed on their board a member of the Chinese Communist Party, which reports to the Chinese Military, thereby giving the Chinese Military all our corporate secrets, patterns, and data. The Chinese unabashedly endeavor to steal patterns and intellectual property without international repercussion in order to make generic, lower-cost brands of every product, including medicines. (Wall Street Journal, "China is National Security Threat No. 1") And as the market supports the lower-priced and generic brands, production in the U.S. diminishes, making the U.S. and the world dependent upon China's production. As a result, in times of competing interests, as with the COVID-19 outbreak in 2020, we found how vulnerable the U.S. can become.

China is also producing 5G Internet Service which has the capacity to surveil and confiscate all data moving across its network. Therefore all public and private institutions using this service are vulnerable to Communist China and the Chinese Military.

China has poured extraordinary sums of money into their huge Navy making them similar in size to the US Navy if not the largest Navy in the world, and they are using this force to dominate countries in the South China Sea and beyond.

Although it's hard to determine exactly how much China is spending on their space program, it appears from their activity that they are spending as much, if not more than the U.S., thereby making our satellites vulnerable to tyranny and our technology in space disadvantaged. As an example, imagine that a farm in Bolivia or a business in South Africa have a choice between satellite internet services that are offered for free by Communist China or for a price from the U.S. or another democratic country. Then imagine how dominance in such an area can shape world opinion as search results suggest that Chinese foreign activities in some area of the world are "liberating" while describing similar US activity as "hostile and imperialistic." Such dominance of critical technology in the hands of a party with ambitions of global dominance is dangerous, just as it is with US companies that seek the same.

We and our way of life are under attack in insidious ways. The attacks are far more subtle than the threats of the Cold Wars and nuclear annihilation. They involve the manipulation of our social thought in our media, entertainment and education toward the values of globalism. They breed elements of discontent, create divisions and conflict, and suggest that harmony in our culture can only occur if we unify in thought and action under one political party.

The attacks are subtle yet pervasive. They are the product of a totalitarian order that destroys the spirit of the individual under the guise of making a better way for all: reducing or eliminating poverty, crime, racism, inequality and injustice all over the world. The propaganda is seductive, as was the offerings of Marx, Lenin, Stalin, Mao, Noriega, Chavez and Castro; however, the true ulterior motive is global domination and the complete subjugation of the person. As the population in the U.S. and around the world grows increasingly poor through inadequate education, a lack of opportunity, and oppressive political policies, their position becomes more popular.

Fortunately we have over 200 years of history that has given us a strong foundation. That foundation is maintaining our country, our institutions, our prosperity, and our Human Rights at present. However, today more than any other time in history, we are being attacked from not only outside opposing forces, but similar forces that have infiltrated our country in our media, universities, corporations, and politics, all of which are eroding this foundation.

We must identify and understand the enemy. Each of the "opposing forces" has the hallmark of controlling the individual and the masses toward its own end. **None of these opposing forces offer freedom of thought, expression, worship or personal protection, which is the criterion that allows one to discern the difference between an ally and an enemy.**

The media has been taken captive by ratings and corporate advertising dollars to the point that all reporting is clearly biased and deceptive toward one direction or another with absolutely no shame or accountability of impartiality. The media does not care what principles it espouses, what incomplete truths or falsities it reports, or what deleterious effect their propaganda has on the public as long as it can garner ratings, advertising dollars and financial support.

They regularly report on the means of overthrowing our country as Anderson Cooper fawns over people like Dr. Cornel West of Harvard University who preaches the failure of the U.S. and capitalism while promoting the redistribution of wealth.

No one media outlet can be trusted regardless of their status as a public or private entity. In order to get any sense of truth, the public must now make the extra effort to scan a variety of contrary media outlets to extrapolate a remote shred of truth. Most people do not make such an effort, and very few make such an effort on a regular basis. Consequently, the masses become indoctrinated with a single, biased viewpoint, without knowing it.

Universities willingly and happily receive millions of dollars from countries that have as their primary goal to overthrow the U.S. and steal our intellectual power. Universities have lost their traditional place as the American institution that embraces free thought and expression to the interests of those who provide funding; consequently, freedom of thought, alternative viewpoints and expression is restricted in the interest of "groupthink" and intellectualism.

Additionally, Marxist revolution is regularly taught in our largest most popular universities: that our capitalistic economy is only favorable to the wealthy few, that our institutions are inherently corrupt, and that the U.S. must be overthrown in order to create an egalitarian system with a single party political system.

The propaganda has filtered down to infiltrate the vulnerable minds of our school children who are being taught anti-American versions of American history: not that the U.S. is "The Great Melting Pot" where it is placed in our Constitution that all people are created equal, but rather that this country was built on institutions that promoted white supremacy and consequently should be destroyed; not that there is equal opportunity for all, but rather that there is a dichotomy of values that favor the rich and powerful versus the common person, and consequently this injustice must be overthrown and equity must be established. These teachings prevail in our schools while straying far from the objective of preparing our children for self-sufficiency in life. The result is a lack of morale at every level of the school system, and overall discontent in our culture. Such a system serves the interest of the oligarchs and totalitarians that benefit from the masses' lack of education, skills and cultural discontent.

Corporations vie for more control of markets and profits at the expense of smaller competitors homogenizing the culture and running competitors out of business. Additionally high tech companies have developed technologies that incorporate anti-competitive exclusions in their software and hardware, while confiscating and collecting information that is useful for their interests but often harmful to the people. Privacy is no longer available to people as either corporations or governments gather data from everyone all the time.

The data collected has one purpose which is to control those from whom the information is collected. Some of the products and services provided may appear to be beneficial to the individual, and consequently the individual might freely surrender their information. Other times, information is taken by various means of high-tech surveillance. Nevertheless, the organization that owns the data has the power to determine how it is used which may or may not be beneficial to the populous.

Politicians are receiving millions of dollars from foreign governments and foreign corporations that have interests contrary to our democratic values. Money can be funneled to private charities and corporations that the politicians own, and the indebtedness to and collusion with dangerous foreign entities are counter to the interests of our country and the citizens of the United States.

Once again, any organization that seeks to control individuals or the masses is acting counter to the interests of our Human Rights. The propaganda is working. We have unwittingly surrendered our freedom to think for ourselves, express ourselves, worship as we wish, and protect ourselves, without comprehending what we are doing. But we feel the problem. There is a tangible sense of rage and frustration that underlies the veil of our civilization. We can sense the erosion of values. We experience the discord in our communities, in our country and in every part of our lives. The erosion has been slow and subtle, even generational, and consequently less apparent, unlike the drastic loss of freedoms in Hong Kong (although it has been accelerated during the COVID-19 crisis).

We are slipping in the wrong direction. As a result, we are becoming ever more anxious about the lack of opportunity and freedom. The solution is not doubling down on the socialist's agenda, seeking security in lieu of freedom. The solution lies in adhering more closely to the values we were founded upon.

Freedom once tasted is never forgotten. Freedom is THE GREATEST motivation of Humankind, even above security, which is what the globalists falsely offer. So again I ask, "Why hasn't anyone done something?!"

4. Our biggest and most grave threats to ourselves inside and outside our country are environmental threats.

Environmental threats include willful neglect and destruction of our natural resources such as our pristine lands, fresh air, clean water and the plant, animal, fungal and bacterial kingdoms, all of which are needed for us to survive, but are under attack by those that seek profit over our lives and wellbeing.

It is absolutely horrible that the air in some places is so poor that one cannot see through the man-made smog, and that people die from chemical contamination of their water supply, and our oceans and lakes are filled with non-biodegradable wastes that are killing our wildlife as well as ourselves. I understand our need for energy to feed and shelter the world's population, but I also understand that we must survive as a species.

Environmental threats may not be as immediate as the other threats I cited above, but they are the greatest threat in the long term as the health of our planet and our species are our ultimate concern. People and organizations that neglect or are complicit in harming the population are as much the enemy as those that seek to control the individual and the masses.

Possibly the gravest threat to our environment and our lives is something that we have not discussed in the media for many years and is quite far from our collective consciousness: our development, use, and disposal of nuclear energy.

We know the devastating effects of nuclear weapons which are still a present threat in our lives today. We tend to neglect this fact, but it is a real danger with nine countries possessing nuclear weapons and others actively pursuing their development.

An equally devastating threat is the widespread development of nuclear energy facilities. We have seen what happened when accidents occurred at Three Mile Island, Chernobyl and Fukushima. Nuclear waste is radioactive not for five or ten years, not for one hundred or one thousand years, but for tens of thousands of years!

There are ninety-eight operating nuclear power plants in the U.S. today and 440 in the world, plus over 200 floating nuclear power plants that power ships.

There are approximately 75,000 nuclear fuel rods in each power plant. (The World Nuclear Association, Nuclear Power Reactors, October 2020) Each of the fuel rods last for about eighteen months and then must be removed from the plant and stored for at least 10,000 years while they remain dangerously radioactive.

Each accident at a nuclear power plant is a major catastrophe that destroys a fifty mile radius for thousands of years to follow. The storage of radioactive uranium is an environmental disaster waiting to happen. How can we continuously and safely store hundreds of thousands of fuel rods without jeopardizing life on our planet? I really don't think we can!

So, I ask once again, "Why hasn't anyone done something?!"

I would like to suggest that when I was younger, I would consider that such problems described above were fodder for the pessimists and the nay-sayers. Today, I realize that each of these issues represent existential threats to you and me, to our country, and in fact, to all of Humankind. I am not presenting these problems to create despair, but rather I am attempting to lay a foundation for possible solutions that will save our planet and Humankind for millennia to come. Solutions that will include resolving these problems to the best of our ability while minimizing collateral damage. That is, not by accepting defeat, shutting down, surrendering our spirit, and ignoring our problems. Not by rioting, looting, and destroying our communities. But rather by engaging all to participate in remedying the problems, utilizing the fantastic resources we have amongst us, offering the public the information, the resources, and the means to resolve these issues, while helping the susceptible and vulnerable who can't help themselves.

The following pages propose solutions.

CHAPTER IV.

Three Elements of Organizations

There are three elements that determine the relationships in all organizations: ownership, decision-making, and compensation. The structure of these elements will determine the quality of the relations.

Traditionally the ownership of an organization is focused in the hands of shareholders. The shareholders make the investment into the organization and receive the dividends and endure the losses.

The decision-makers of any organization are determined in its charter. They are the ones who are responsible for determining the direction of each matter related to the organization, including all financial decisions and policy matters.

Those that are involved with the organization are compensated in a manner that the decision-makers determine, and those that are offered the compensation can decide if they wish to be part of the organization or not based on the compensation offered.

In the United State of America, the Founding Parents made each citizen a SHAREHOLDER of the United States of America. We the People are essentially the owners of the organization we call the United States Government. Our investment is being a committed citizen of the United States who will protect and contribute to the government. The return on our investment is the enjoyment of the bounty and the hardships of the failures.

The Founding Parents also made the US citizen the DECISION-MAKERS in our government. We The People determine the direction of the matters related to our governance. However, they also made a system that included representatives of the people to act on behalf of the people. The officials the people elect are responsible for implementation of the decisions determined by the people since all of whom make the decisions cannot logistically be involved with each detail and since the detail of each decision is laborious in its fulfillment. The elected officials are NOT responsible for making decisions FOR the people, but rather IN SERVICE OF THE PEOPLE. Thus, the brilliance of a Democratic Republic. Nevertheless, the citizens are ultimately responsible for making all financial decisions related to the government's income and expenses, and all policy decisions that affect the rights and conditions of the people.

The compensation of the people who work in government is determined by the Decision-Makers, who are the people. Therefore the ultimate determination of the compensation of each government employee, elected or hired, must be determined by We the People.

These facts are the foundation of everything that follows in this book. It is a radical concept that places the power in the hands of We the People as intended by the genius of our Founding Parents. This concept turns on its head the formation of every government ever in existence, giving the people the power, governing from the bottom up, rather than from the top down. The sad truth is that despite the charter of our Founding Documents, We the People have relinquished control to politicians, special interest groups, the one-percenters, the media, a few corporations, technocrats, and the power brokers in our country. The angst we feel is a result of the improper relationships we have in our organization called government. If we are ever to fulfill the charter of our Founding Parents, we must fully realize their vision. It is our obligation to rectify these relationships and realize the charter of our Founding Parents more fully.

The example of social change by Martin Luther King, Jr. is an excellent illustration of progress toward the charge we've been given in our US Constitution. We must remember that we live in the greatest country the world has ever known, despite significant faults and shortcomings, and that each generation's charge is to make this country ever-greater, manifesting the vision of our Founding Parents within our system, which itself provides a peaceful and civil means for change. All the problems that threaten our country today are answered if we return to study and fulfill the vision of our Founding Parents. Manifesting our founding charter will save our country for centuries, even millennia to come, as well as lead the world toward peace and prosperity.

Conflicts between unions/workers and management/ownership can be reduced to the structures of the same three organizational elements and will be discussed later in this book.

CHAPTER V.

Manifesting the Charge of Our Founding Parents

Since 1776, the United States of America has been the leading proponent of Human Rights. The U.S. is the first country in history that was created and had incorporated into its charter principles that the citizens can think for themselves, express themselves freely, worship as they wish and protect themselves and their families rather than have tyrannical rulers determine such for the people. As a result, the people of the United States have enjoyed a development in 244 years that the world has never seen. Extraordinary advances in medicine, technology, science, education, longevity and life-style have been made because of the respect and freedom the free enterprise system has afforded the people. And as the democratic values of the U.S. spread throughout the world, the people of the world benefited from better living standards.

But along with the benefits we have enjoyed come the challenges that result from breaking new ground. We are just children in our growth to real-ize the principles of our Founding Parents to respect all people as equally created individuals and to treat each person equally under the law.

These founding principles required us us to resolve cultural conflicts that have existed throughout the history of civilization. Consequently, our nation was torn in civil war as it endeavored to abolish slavery in the 1800s, remove Jim Crow laws in the 1900s, and extinguish intimidation and oppression that limit human rights and opportunity of minorities up to the present. The Civil Rights Movement in the United States continues to act to eliminate remnants of racism in our culture and in our institutions. Unlike any other country in the world, Affirmative Action Laws have been instituted to ensure that minorities would receive comparable benefits in admissions to schools and public institutions as well as in employment opportunities.

We have led and championed the Women's Suffrage Movement and recently celebrated 100 years of women's right to vote and equally share in the political process. We are still engaged in removing obstacles to equal opportunity for women.

We have been leaders in accepting the Lesbian, Gay, Bisexual, Transsexual/ Transgender and Queer (LGBTQ) community into all sectors of our country and providing equal treatment under the law, as we have been charged to accept that all people have been created equally.

It must be noted that respect for the individual and the rights to freely express oneself, worship, and protect oneself does not include taxation or represent a financial burden on the citizenry. Rights are codified into law to ensure that oppression is removed and expunged under the law. Rights never include taxation.

Codifying into law the Human Rights of the individual gave the US citizen an autonomy or sovereignty over its being. The right to own private property is an extension of this autonomy. Private property is legalized through deed, title, trademark, copyright, patents and the like.

Freedom from oppression does not bring with it impunity. Human Rights allow a person to act without being discriminated against, without being stopped from expressing oneself, from worshiping, or from protecting oneself and one's property. However, living in freedom includes a responsibility to act without imparting harm to others. Engaging in behavior that harms others has consequences.

Our lawmakers have generally determined what degree of harm is unlawful. Usually perpetration of physical harm to an individual, group or to property is unacceptable and legal consequences follow. On the other hand, a full range of thought is acceptable without legal repercussion; although intellectual property is protected.

Therefore, minority citizens, women and the LBGTQ community have the right to express themselves, worship, protect themselves and their families, and participate equally in the political process along with all US citizens. All citizens are also responsible for adhering to the laws of the governments, engaging in legal trade and earning status and a lifestyle based on behaviors, character, and merit.

Preferential treatments of minorities and women are a reaction to the centuries of oppression and maltreatment. However, such partiality must be limited as movements to overcompensate for wrongs in the past only create additional wrongs of the opposite character.

Therefore political and legal decisions cannot continue to be made on the basis of the color of one's skin, one's sex or sexuality, place of origin, or any other defining label. Rather, political and legal decisions must be made on the basis of merit and character in order to transcend the partiality given to parts of a person, thereby reverting to equal justice and opportunity for all under the law.

This standard must be applied to people who engage in the destruction of fetuses under the laws of freedom of choice. Having the right to choose does not include the right to physically harm another and such behavior must be held accountable. Sixty million abortions have taken place in the United States of America, making this action the largest act of genocide and eugenics in our history. It is a moral disaster and a massive legal mistake that is perpetuated by enormous financial incentives. The money spent on abortions could easily be provided to adoption services instead.

Rights do not carry with it taxation. Therefore healthcare is NOT A RIGHT as Senator Bernie Sanders contends. Rights are freedom from oppression, not an agreement of the citizenry to provide a service.

The Founding Principles of the United States include a Bill of Rights that allows its people to live freely and protect themselves with equal treatment under the law. It is a governing system of the people, by the people, for the people. Any additional programs enacted by the Federal Government are social programs that are funded by taxpayers' dollars and therefore must be decided upon by the taxpayer. So, let's look at how closely these values have been instituted over the 244 years of our nation's existence.

Every year the Executive Branch proposes a spending bill that recommends spending in twelve sectors of our government, managed by subcommittees. The recommendations are sent to the legislature who may approve, amend, or revise the recommendations. The end result is twelve Appropriation Bills which fund our government. This money essentially ensures the performance of government services over the following twelve months. Without funding, regardless of law, services are not provided. Therefore, let's focus on what the government controls, how much control We the People have, and how much control we have conceded.

Listed below are the twelve subcommittees and the amounts funded in 2019. I included the percentage of the expenditure against total expenditures as per the Congressional Budget Office (2019) https://www.cbo.gov/topics/budget/status-appropriations.

Name of Subcommittee	FY2019 amount (% of all government expenditures)
Agriculture, Rural Development, and Food and Drug Administration	$23.0 billion (0.57%)
Commerce, Justice, and Science	$64.1 billion (1.59%)
Defense	$606.5 billion (15.06%)
Energy and Water Development	$44.6 billion (1.11%)
Financial Services and General Government (includes Judicial Branch, the Executive Office of the President, and District of Columbia appropriations)	$23.4 billion (0.58%)
Homeland Security	$49.4 billion (1.23%)
Interior and Environment	$35.6 billion (0.88%)
Labor, Health and Human Services, and Education	$178.1 billion (4.42%)
Legislative Branch	$4.8 billion (1.19%)
Military Construction and Veterans Affairs	$97.1 billion (2.41%)

State and Foreign Operations	$46.2 billion (1.15%)
Transportation and Housing and Urban Development	$71.1 billion (1.76%)

You will notice that the total amount spent on the twelve sectors of government equals $1243.9 billion which amounts to 30.89% of US Expenditures in 2019. This amount is called Discretionary Spending. The remainder is spent on Mandatory Spending which includes the following:

Name	FY2019 amount
Social Security Administration	$1,041 billion (25.85%)
Medicare	$645 billion (16.02%)
Medicaid	$419 billion (10.4%)
Supplemental Security Income, Housing Assistance, Other Programs	$672 billion (16.69%)

~The US total spending (which includes additional emergency spending) for Fiscal Year 2019 was $4.4 trillion.

~The total US income for FY 2019 was $3.5 trillion, which means the U.S. overspent about $1.1 trillion, which is 31.4% of US expenditures. This amount was added to the US National Debt.

~The negative cash flow of the Social Security Program is about $100 billion.

~The interest paid on the National Debt in 2019 was $574 billion (https://www.treasurydirect.gov/govt/reports/ir/ir_expense.htm).

(Please visit www.MarkABuzzotta.com for annual updates.)

So given this information, we need to ask ourselves a few relevant questions.

CHAPTER VI.

Relevant Questions and Answers

First, does it seem that the people charged with making a budget and spending our tax dollars are doing their job? Or doing a good job?

Well, as a common citizen of the U.S., it seems to me that I cannot establish a budget and then increase it by 31% and essentially spend 1.26% of my income, and go deeper into debt year after year. I have to balance my checkbook, balance my budget and be fiscally responsible. Even if I run up my credit cards and borrow from every source available, my spending is limited.

Not the US government! The politicians that are able to get money into their voting districts generally get elected and reelected. The powers in Washington have no concern for the fiscal stability of this country. Doling out favors and engaging in reckless abandon when spending what the politicians seem to think is an endless resource of taxpayer's money is horribly unacceptable! Politicians from every party pander to the people promising all sorts of incentives and government benefits to get support and votes. The result is a National Debt of over $25 trillion dollars, which is over seven times the annual income of the United States! It is far, far more than any borrowing standard in the private sector, and it places an ADDITIONAL tax burden on every citizen in the U.S! There is no accountability, no overseeing body, and no legislation that prevents the abuses. So it continues.

My grade is an "F." The politicians have failed in their job and they have FAILED us in managing the checkbook of the United States!

Second, why is the government managing and funding the Social Security Program?

Granted, I believe most people in the U.S. would agree that the Social Security Program is a good idea. In fact, when Roosevelt created the program, it boosted the morale of the people and the US economy. It was a great idea. However, the implementation of this idea has significant problems. The people that contribute to the Social Security Fund are the US workers. The people who receive the benefits are the people who are retired and for the most part, no longer working. As the lifespan of Americans increase and the retired population exceeds the number in the workforce, a problem occurs. The structure of the program begins to resemble an inverted pyramid where more people begin to receive benefits than the amount of money that is being put into the system. Therefore, the US government, i.e., the taxpayer, has to fund the program or the government has to borrow more money to pay its obligations.

Notice that the Social Security Administration receives the largest percentage of taxpayer dollars, by far. However, once again, without any over-sight or accountability, lawmakers have mismanaged it. They borrow against it and are paying large sums of money in interest on the debt. They misdirect funds and employ "creative" accounting practices in order to receive, manage, and control the money.

The concept of providing security for people who have worked a certain number of years and may not be able to work as they reach an older age, and providing for those that are disabled, is a good idea. **Good ideas, however, are limited by reality in that they must be funded and managed responsibly.** The government should **NOT** be managing the program. The government may authorize the program, set up the program, determine the amount taken from each paycheck, and regulate it, but not manage the program. In other words, the program should be privatized. The retirement savings should be placed in the worker's own fund, NOT held and managed by the government!

A privatized Social Security Program could be constructed similar to the current system in that deductions from the worker's pay can be equally matched by the employer up to a certain amount. Currently, the worker contributes 6.2% of his/her check up to $137,700 per year in earnings and the employer matches that amount. But in a privatized system, the money would be managed and owned by the worker -- with limitations to prevent withdrawals till retirement age and prevent mismanaging the funds so that the funds will be preserved. Criteria and regulations would be necessary just as with IRAs, 401Ks and SEP plans.

However, the government has no right to hold the funds and use it for its own purposes as it's the people's money. If the government had any interest in securing the privatized program, it could insure each individual's fund similar to the way the FDIC insures deposits in banks. But the government should have no more control. Not only is it outside the purview of the government to be in the pension fund business, but the government cannot be trusted to manage the funds properly. Let me explain in detail with examples.

If a citizen works at least ten years cumulatively, he/she is eligible to receive Social Security benefits at age sixty-two or over. To simplify the calculations, the worker will receive approximately 8% per year of the total amount of tax paid over his/her work life if he/she retires at sixty-two, and a little less than 12% per year if he/she retires at sixty-seven. The benefits will last for the remainder of the person's life.

On average, a worker and his/her employer(s) together pay over $300,000 in taxes to the Social Security Administration over the course of their work-life. But for sake of simplicity, let's use $100,000 in career taxes paid.

So, for example, if a worker and his/her employer(s) pay a total of $100,000 in taxes over the course of the worker's work-life, the retiree can expect between $8000 per year (if retired at sixty-two years of age) to about $12,000 per year (if retired at sixty-seven).

The life expectancy of a man that retires today at sixty-seven is about 16.5 years (eighty-three years old) and for a woman is 21 years (eighty-eight years old). That means that the SSA will on average pay between $132,000 and $252,000 in retirement benefits to each retired worker for every $100,000 in taxes paid.

On the surface, that doesn't appear to be a bad deal for the worker. And it looks like the government is losing money on the average amount of benefits paid. But look deeper.

If a worker and the employer took the same amount of taxes and put it in a fund that generated just 5% compounded annually over the course of their work-life, the $100,000 in taxes paid would actually approximate $165,000 in twenty years and $603,000 over forty years! In other words, the Social Security Administration is not losing any money on the taxes paid into the system versus the benefits paid out. In fact, they are profiting a significant amount! And again, remember, this example is based on paying just $100,000 in taxes over a worker's work-life. (You may find your personal Social Security benefits and other details at www.SSA.gov.) The taxed amount is usually two to four times this amount! The amount of money the Social Security Administration and the US government is making on our money is astounding.

There is more to this story....The reason the SSA may go bankrupt in a few years without adjustments to the amounts they tax us is that the money a worker pays into the system is not directed to the retirement benefits he/she receives. In other words, the 6.2% that the worker pays to the Social Security Administration plus the matching amount the employer pays goes into a fund that is used to pay the people that are retired and qualify for benefits under the regulations of the Social Security Program. So, as the pool of retirees increases, and the life-span of retirees in the U.S. increase, the work-pool is stressed, cash flow becomes negative and a greater burden is placed on the government (the taxpayer) to pay the obligated benefits. Additionally, if for any reason, the workforce pool decreases, more stress is placed on the system as less money is placed into the Social Security Fund. Therein is the problem with having the government manage a pension program. The principles are simply not sound.

Granted, in defense of Roosevelt and those that created the program, setting up the system where the current workers contribute to a fund from which the retirees benefit could take place immediately. In other words, nearly as quickly as the program was instituted, retirees could begin receiving benefits, which was important to help the U.S. to emerge from the Great Depression. However, no suitable long range plan was instituted that resolved inherent problems which we are suffering from today.

A. The system is threatened with bankruptcy if Congress doesn't increase the required amount of tax payments to fund the program. The taxpayers must pay any deficits so that the U.S. can pay its obligations, or the shortages are paid by additional borrowing thereby increasing the National Debt, which of course, is ultimately the taxpayers' problem.

B. Congress uses the equity in the Social Security Fund to borrow against with interest so that they can pay other obligations and expenditures.

C. The size of the Social Security Fund is so large, over $1 trillion, that it may become a resource in the event the U.S. experiences catastrophe and needs emergency financing. That possibility jeopardizes the sweat equity of each worker that paid into the fund for all of their working careers. That horrible possibility could reduce or eliminate Social Security payments to retirees and the disabled. Such a liability should not even be a possibility!

D. Despite the amount of money that we workers have paid into the system, we have no control of, access to or ownership of the funds. The policy makers that instituted the Social Security Administration made it such. Whereas, if the funds were privatized, we could control our funds, decide on the withdrawal amounts of the funds, and bequeath the funds to our heirs, while benefiting from the extraordinary amount of growth that takes place as the funds compound over years and years.

Essentially, we have been deprived of the wealth that we earned while the government has squandered and mismanaged the funds that we have provided. Additionally, those that seek to garner the power of government over the people have essentially stolen our birthright, or better said, our citizen-right. We must change these institutions, not violently, but rather through the means available to us in the political system.

This last point (D) is worth elaborating upon.

As shown in the example above, compound interest over the work-life of the worker, which can be as low as ten years to over fifty years, creates extraordinary wealth. The average worker would have well over $1,000,000 by retirement age if the required contributions are kept the same as they are now (6.2% of the worker's pay and a matching amount by the employer). If this fund was privatized so the contributions are managed similar to the rules already in place for IRA, 401K and SEP accounts, then the worker would have a nice "nest egg" and a secure retirement. Retirees could possibly live off 5% withdrawals and the principle would be preserved if the fund maintained an average of at least 5% growth.

Again, this scenario is quite realistic as the payments are already happening; they are just going to the Social Security Administration and the government is mismanaging the money and squandering it!

This money would increase the amounts invested in stocks, bonds, notes and bank accounts and increase the size of financial institutions everywhere the money is invested. The lending and investment power of these financial institutions would increase significantly. The stock market would grow massively, and most importantly, the personal wealth of each individual would be fantastic, while creating legacies bequeathed to following generations or donated as desired.

Individuals would have control over where they placed their money, just as they have control now over the places they put their other retirement funds. In addition to stocks, bonds, notes and savings, they can opt for annuities. Some annuities offer higher guaranteed interest rates than bank savings accounts and/or guaranteed income for life or for a specified period, with conditions. Nevertheless, the individual could make these decisions, again, within the constraints of similar regulations that limit withdrawals to 59.5 years of age, borrowing conditions, etc.

And if the government felt that privatization was too risky in that there is a possibility that money might be squandered by individuals that might make bad investment decisions, then limitations can be placed on the first $250,000 which would be held in secure accounts, or insurance on the first $250,000 could be provided by the government or required to be purchased by the individual so that amount is secure similar to the FDIC insurance program on bank deposits.

Again, this could all happen if the Social Security Program was simply privatized and controlled in a fashion as other existing pension plans. It would revolutionize the income disparities in the U.S. It would virtually eliminate the lower-end communities all over the U.S. It would incentivize people to work rather than collect unemployment, welfare benefits or other social programs that dis-incentivize work. It would increase the number of products, services and opportunities all over our country as the financial institutions would finance new ideas and businesses. It could virtually make the U.S. self-sufficient in manufacturing products that are made in other countries. It would increase competition in all fields thereby creating the best regulation of the economy naturally, without government intervention, as free enterprise encourages companies to provide products and services that improve upon the status quo, and often at better prices. It would give citizens a sense that they are invested in this country as they can see a direct relationship between working in the U.S. and developing true wealth during their lifetime. And it would settle immigration issues in that the volume of immigrants can be determined by the number of workers that are needed or not needed to perpetuate the economy.

The government would change from being a pension fund manager to manager of the country's true government responsibilities and our free enterprise system, while eliminating a massive negative cash flow and tax burden for the citizens.

So I ask you, who do you think can manage your retirement money better, you or the federal government? I believe the answer is obvious!

<u>Transition to Privatizing Social Security</u>

Making the transition from the current system to privatization poses some logistical problems. I will try to delineate the problems along with possible solutions. Certainly accountants, actuaries and others learned in this matter would offer more expert knowledge in making the transition; however, I'll outline the general principles and the process.

Calculating the amount of money that each retiree would have in his/her fund is relatively simple.

Records of how much money has been paid into the system by each worker and the amounts paid by each worker's employers are available. The fund of each worker would be determined by compounding the amount in the worker's fund each year at 5%. The total is the amount of money that the worker would own. This information would be a reference point only.

Workers and their employers just entering the workforce would contribute to their own fund throughout their work-life and at retirement time would have their funds available to them just as is the case with other retirement funds currently in place, like IRA, 401K and SEP accounts.

However, currently, workers and their employers are contributing to the current Social Security Program, which means that their contributions are going to retirees rather than into the workers' own funds. The retirees are entitled to the money since they played by the rules all of their careers and deserve the money. It's certainly not their fault that the government set up a faulty system, and they shouldn't be penalized in any way. They need to continue to get their Social Security benefits as promised. So here's a solution.

For the sake of simplicity, I will suggest that one's work-life is about fifty years, from seventeen years of age to sixty-seven years of age. The new workers who will contribute to their own fund are excluded from the overall pool of workers contributing to the traditional SSA each year, which means that 2% of the workers are not contributing to the current system and each following year an additional 2% of the workforce would not contribute until all the workers are out of the old system in fifty years.

That means that every year, using current numbers, the SSA would lose about $22 billion per year in revenue collected. So in ten years, there would theoretically be 20% less money (or $220 billion) in the current system to pay retirees, and in twenty years, there would be 40% ($440 billion) less money, and so on so that in fifty years the current Social Security System fund would be empty. This scenario would occur if no adjustments were made to the amounts paid into the system and the work pool stayed the same as it is now. Consequently, retirees would receive progressively less benefits till the system is exhausted when retirees would receive nothing.

In 2020, the regulations are that workers pay 6.2% up to $137,700 per year in income, and employers match that amount, while the self-employed pay 12.4%. No tax is paid over that maximum income amount and the maximum limit is raised each year. However, if the United States removed any income limit and required all who file Individual Income Tax Returns to pay into the system similarly, an additional $500 billion dollars would be paid into the system every year. (https://www.irs.gov/statistics/soi-tax-stats-individual-statistical-tables-by-size-of-adjusted-gross-income) And there would be no risk that retirees' benefits would be jeopardized.

That suggestion appears to be a fair and simple solution to keep the system solvent for the next thirty years. Theoretically, the overage that would be paid into the current system during the first thirty years could be saved with compound interest to have the necessary funds for the remaining twenty years of transition.

Notice that the way the system is set up now is that high income earners (over $137,700/year), are allowed to keep their own money and can decide how to use it themselves. It is not taken from them by the government and then used however the government determines. Personally, I am in favor of mandatory saving, so I believe the contributions to the retirement funds should be legislated. However, I believe the worker newly entering the workforce should be contributing 5% to their retirement fund with the employer matching it or 10% for the self-employed.

So, let's summarize.

1. Taxes could go down for workers and the employers in the new system of privatized retirement funding after the transition to privatization is completed.

2. Retirement savings would grow at extraordinary rates using the power of compound reinvestment over time.

3. Each American worker would accumulate well over $1,000,000 in retirement savings in their working lifetime, allowing the worker to OWN his retirement fund and decide how his/her funds are invested.

4. The private fund makes the worker vested in the U.S. This action will make the worker committed to the U.S., morale and patriotism will naturally grow and crime is likely to diminish.

5. Each American worker is likely to invest their funds in the U.S. by purchasing real estate, equities, and other personal items of interest, thereby increasing commitment to the U.S. via ownership of private property. The likelihood is that people will invest in their homes and communities and the development of all communities will be raised, minimizing the likelihood of poor communities and neighborhoods.

6. An incentive to work will override incentives to receive benefits from social programs. Social benefits provided by the US government would be reduced as the wealth of the nation's people increase.

7. Investing this money in the economy would give the U.S. an opportunity to expand at phenomenal rates.

8. The U.S. could immediately remove the negative cash flow of the Social Security Administration thereby taking a burden off the government and the taxpayer.

9. The US government would get out of the retirement fund business which it has no justifiable reason to be in, and theoretically could manage their current responsibilities better.

10. The taxpayer is not at risk of losing their retirement benefits, and the taxpayer is not likely to have imposed upon them an increase to pay for Social Security benefits.

11. The US government is not as likely to redirect, borrow against, mismanage or confiscate the Social Security Fund.

It's time to make the transition. If it's government of the people, by the people, for the people, then we should be making these decisions regarding OUR money! We the People have the means and the ability. So I ask, "Are we going to do something?!"

We need to enact legislative changes now, or vote people into power that will make the changes. Violence and destruction are not the answer.... We have the BEST system in the world at present. However, we are a far cry from realizing the values we have been charged to manifest.

Third question...Where is the rest of our tax money going?

The US Budget for Discretionary Spending in 2019 was $1.244 trillion and Mandatory Spending was $2.777 trillion, totaling (with interest payments) $4.4 trillion. The US government is the largest organization in the world and in history. We know how difficult it is for two people to agree on any one matter, or even for a small organization to agree on one or several matters. It is understandably difficult to obtain a majority or a super majority or any agreement among 435 Representatives plus 100 Senators and the President, all of whom are from diverse backgrounds, varied cultures and different parts of the U.S.

Managing a $1,000,000,000 company like the National Football League is difficult itself. Managing a $4.4 trillion organization, the largest in the world, is extraordinary!

However, there are certain activities that the government is simply not qualified to manage. For example, the US government is not qualified to build US fighter jets so it accepts bids from US companies who propose to build the jets for the U.S. Same is true for government buildings and other structures. The U.S. announces its interest in having a particular project completed and it seeks competitive bids from several companies. Often incentives and penalties are included in the acceptance of a bid which ensures the performance required.

Similarly, the government has no qualifications to be involved with many other projects that it is not qualified to develop, manage or maintain.

The Social Security Administration is one of the projects the U.S. government should not control. It was a great idea presented by President Roosevelt in a time of need, however, implementation and management of the program is fraught with corruption and mismanagement. The pension fund of the US citizenry should be privatized immediately!

The Transportation System in the U.S. is another program that the government is not qualified to manage and maintain.

Here are a couple of examples before I make my point. The Big Dig was a massive highway construction project in Boston that began in 1991 at a budgeted cost of $3 billion. It was finally completed in 2007 with cost overruns that amounted to $22 billion! Corruption and delays were neglected by each successive administration while the taxpayers footed the bill. No one was accountable.

In March of 2017, a bridge near downtown Atlanta on Interstate Highway 85 collapsed causing gridlock all over the heavily crowded roads of Atlanta. The US Department of Transportation and the Georgia Department of Transportation said it would take at least a year to fix the bridge and restore highway traffic to the pre-collapse levels. Needless to say, metro Atlanta motorists were horrified at the prospect of enduring a year of gridlock. The intangible economic cost to the city would be enormous as all commercial activity as well as personal travel would be nearly impossible. The Mayor called the event a "transportation crisis" and the Governor declared a state of emergency.

The solution was to contract the redevelopment of the bridge to a private firm. Bids were accepted and C.W. Matthews Contracting Company promised to have the bridge restored in two and a half months. The Georgia DOT oversaw the project and gave a $3 million bonus for successful completion of the project early. The bridge collapsed on March 30 and it was restored with traffic flowing better than before the disaster on May 12, over a month early!

The fact of the matter is that ANYTHING the government undertakes is fraught with extensions, cost overruns and overall mismanagement, particularly because the politicians that oversee all processes of the government are not held accountable. There are no financial repercussions for overspending and mismanagement other than being voted out of office. Ultimately the taxpayer has to bear the burden of such continuous problems while the inattentive, unproductive politician is gone. Multiply this example by the actions of governments of cities all over the U.S., by the governments of all fifty States and territories, and by every level and office of government for years and years. The result is that we have over $25 trillion in debt and an economy that slows down to little or no growth. We have burdens placed on taxpayers to pay for past problems and increasing new costs, while fostering a new generation that has little to no opportunity to realize their dreams. Is there really any wonder why the younger generation is frustrated and rebellious?

Governments on every level, national, state, and local, should take the money allotted to the Department of Transportation and request bids from private companies to redevelop, maintain, and manage the roadways. Private companies would be responsible for doing exactly what the DOT requires at a preset contracted amount within a specific time frame. And if the job is not done as contracted then penalties are instituted with the ultimate option to hire a better contractor.

The same can be done for the train system, the airports, public transportation, and waterways. The government should take the money that's budgeted for each transportation service, and have private companies bid for the work in specified regions, while overseeing the performance of each job. Not only will each service be managed better in the private sector, but the government will no longer be involved with performing jobs and projects it cannot manage properly. Relief will be given to governments on all levels as well as to the taxpayer, and accountability would naturally be incorporated into the system.

Education is another area where the government has no expertise. Once again, there are not many people that would dispute the validity of this social program; however, there are many other people that are far better trained and more knowledgeable than the government employees who run our public school systems.

Our public schools are failing. Morale in the schools is low and the dropout rate is very high (https://nces.ed.gov/fastfacts/display.asp?id=16), and 15% never graduate (https://educationdata.org/high-school-dropout-rate/). Students lose interest and become frustrated as they are force fed information that is often irrelevant to their lives and future work careers.

Public schools are generally financed by property taxes that amount to about 85% of one's total property tax bill. The total amount of money spent in 2016-17 was $739 billion (https://nces.ed.gov/fastfacts/display.asp?id=66). The federal government contributed over $81 billion dollars to education in 2019 per the US Department of Education (https://www2.ed.gov/about/overview/budget/tables.html?src=rt).

This massive amount of funding on all levels is only exceeded by additional money that is thrown at the educational system every time national standardized scores fall or rankings against other countries slip, or other issues befall the system.

Once again, privatizing the educational system would improve the system drastically. The money that is already allotted to each community and each school system can be used to award funding to the organizations that offer the best schools in a fiscally responsible manner. The government can take the money that is given to the schools that have the poorest performance on all measures (graduation rates, SAT scores, attendance, etc.) and request bids for a new privately owned school with high academic standards that will operate within the financial boundaries allotted. Private schools will always perform better than public schools in the same community. Private schools hold children accountable to academic and behavior standards that public schools cannot. They do not have to be homogenized and can offer specialization in certain areas like science, math or technical development. They can begin to teach more world skills that are relevant to their lives such as sustainable living (i.e., housing, elementary farming, food supply, nutrition, safety, and socialization skills). They can offer apprenticeships and internships in areas students may want to explore as careers. These programs would also stimulate the local economies as businesses obtain free labor in return for teaching student-apprentices a skill, trade, or craft that are practical and relevant.

The government can finance the development of private schools while maintaining certain academic standards by having annual standardized tests that determine advancement and eventual graduation of the students. This process of privatizing our schools would not cost the taxpayer any additional money and would remove the government from their ineptness in a field they are not qualified to manage. More discussion of the privatization of education will be discussed in a later chapter.

The Food & Drug Administration Budget was $5.7 billion in 2019 (https://www.fda.gov/about-fda/fda-basics/fact-sheet-fda-glance). I would venture to say that the government could outsource the same services to US companies and get more accomplished quicker than government-run operations. Again, the private sector has an incentive to be more streamlined; it is held to standards of accountability, and will do the work at a competitive price, and do it all without partisan politics. I believe that we could have two or three times the amount of services provided by the private sector than is now provided by the current FDA.

The Post Office is subsidized at a rate of over $18 billion a year by the taxpayers (https://fortune.com/2015/03/27/us-postal-service/). Private, independent companies should evaluate what services are beneficial and what services should be eliminated, and recommendations can be submitted to the government. The government can then determine what services it finds essential and can open competitive bids to provide the services desired. Contracts can be given on a limited basis, i.e., five years or so at a time, while the government oversees the efficiency of the services. Overall, private companies will provide better services at lower rates, and bailouts could be eliminated. Additionally one of the biggest costs of the US Postal Service -- pensions -- can be eliminated with the privatized Social Security Program cited earlier.

The budget of the Environmental Protection Agency was $8.8 billion in 2019 (https://www.epa.gov/planandbudget/budget). Rather than managing its own department, the agency can take competitive bids from private companies that are more likely to provide the services at lower prices, without delays and with far less politicization. For $8.8 billion a year, there can be two or three companies or more that provide identical services so that cross referencing of data can be provided, rather than from just one source.

Homeland Security, Water and Energy Development, Housing and Urban Development and other agencies all can be privatized with the use of competitive bidding, proper government oversight and incentives and penalties incorporated into the contracts to ensure performance. Additionally, given the enormous current budgets provided to each agency, contracts can be given to more than one company within the oversight of each agency in order to develop competition between companies and also provide confirmation of studies and information.

Overall, many of the agencies of the US government can be privatized in order to improve efficiency, eliminate cost overruns, create a system of accountability, and reduce partisan political pressure while minimizing the burden on the government and the taxpayer. The government sets standards (as voiced by the people), finances the agencies and various projects, and provides oversight, but it is not involved with the functions of the agency. Politics in government agencies is eliminated while the free market propels efficiency.

For years, it was believed that government run agencies would provide services purely motivated to fulfill the interest of the people whereas private companies would be less reliable because they are driven by profit. History has proven otherwise. The mismanagement of government agencies with cost overruns, delays and overall inefficiency due to lack of accountability has proven that the government is not capable to perform its assigned duties without corruption. Free market forces naturally eliminate these problems through competitive bidding and corporate accountability, while oversight can be maintained by government officials who are elected or appointed by elected officials. It is a proven fact that private organizations are far more efficient than public organizations.

Current politicians will be averse to the movement toward privatization of the services cited above due to the fact that they would lose extraordinary power. Favors and appointments would be eliminated and the powerbrokers in Washington and all government offices would be left without influence. Strong push back against privatization should be expected as this movement is one of We the People against those that have taken the power from the people. However, the only way We the People can take and keep control is through removal of centralized systems and reliance upon the free market.

The free market has an intelligence that cannot be replicated by any form of centralization. Power placed in the hands of any person or group cannot match the wisdom of market forces. The market is a living force that collectively gathers intelligence from all sources available (all people, all conditions), and moves naturally. Sometimes, we do not have the insight to understand the movements of the free market, but that does not mean that there isn't wisdom in the movements. It just means that we don't understand the movement. Nevertheless, the value of each collective move eventually becomes clear, sometimes with hindsight.

The market always prevails in the long run in any case. Centralization only delays the inevitable. Instituting centralized controls, allotting power to individuals and groups, and all attempts to change the tide of the market, are only temporary measures that lose to the more powerful force of nature in the long run.

So how do we tap into this force, this collective power we describe as the Market? **People** are the answer. We the People are the force that drives the economy, the government, and the world. It's the inherent intelligence in the Free Market as found in the will of the People that is the most powerful force on the planet. Greater than any planned economy. Greater than any form of noble efforts to design a fair egalitarian system. Greater than any scientific or academic control. And even more intelligent than any form of developed artificial intelligence. Nothing can match the power, resource and genius of the Free Market. NOTHING!

It outlasts regulation and institutions as the Market cannot be extinguished. It survives centralization and socialist's movements because the spirit of the People cannot be destroyed and eventually wins. It reigns supreme regardless of all constraints and proves its dominance like Nature itself which cannot be conquered.

So, how can we create a system where the We the People make our voices heard? Voting once every couple of years certainly is not working. WWOFPD? (What Would Our Founding Parents Do?)

Communication is the answer. Let's explore...

CHAPTER VII.

Tyranny Versus Freedom

Every few years, politicians run for elected positions in the government. They must raise money which they use to influence public opinion and win more votes. The money which comes from people and corporations is so massive that the politicians have no choice but to be responsive to those that finance their elections. So, pandering to the people and corporations become the norm for elected officials, and a greater priority than their obligation to serve the People.

It can be argued as it has been in the courts that money is just the expression of the interests of people and the companies that support the elected officials, and that the elected officials have a responsibility to represent the interest of those that have placed them in office. That argument is perfectly justified.

However, inevitable conflict occurs when hundreds of lawmakers get together to enact or try to enact legislation. In such a collective environment, respect and dignity for each position must be maintained, but is often lost in this day and age. Such respect and dignity for each individual in the collective, as well as to the collective legislative body, must be greater than the interests of the parts (the special interest factions) and the money that has placed them in office.

But unfortunately, the system is such that it discourages respect to the institution they represent, the other lawmakers, and We the People in favor of the money that has financed their elections.

Our elected officials have lost the value of the whole. They are disregarding the extraordinary history that has made the United States the "City on the Hill" for the entire world for generations, while the interests of a few and the most powerful who support the electorate take precedent.

It can be argued, once again, that the few who have become more educated, more knowledgeable, and more experienced, have an enlightened perspective which could benefit the greater whole if their influence was extended and their positions institutionalized. However, history has proven that rule by an intellectual class or any centralized body, however enlightened, to be a failure.

The Communist regimes of the USSR, China, Cuba, Venezuela and others promised better societies by taking money from the rich and sharing the wealth with the poor. They promised humanitarian care for each individual and a massive reduction of crime and violence through the implementation of an egalitarian society. These are noble values that propelled the leaders of these movements as inspired by Marx.

However, in order to implement such societies, all Human Rights have to be removed as individuals' natural inclination to problem-solve, create, and grow is destroyed in the interest of the State's values to homogenize the culture and remove personal ambitions.

Thoughts, values and expressions that are contrary to the stated values of the system are repressed so that the State's values prevail. Books, churches, and groups expressing ideas contrary to the State are eliminated. Free speech, freedom of expression, freedom of worship, freedom of the press and freedom to protect oneself and one's personal views are eliminated. Private property is eliminated and all wealth is owned by the government. Consequently millions upon millions of people were killed in the interest of creating the utopian societies promised by Marx and his devotees -- Lenin, Stalin, Mao, Noriega, Chavez, and Castro among others.

Between one-third and one-half of the world's people were subjected to tyrannical systems that proposed a better life on the planet, but in fact brought the world to near total destruction.

At the essence of the problem is the misconception of the individual's value. Once respect for the individual's inherent intelligence is lost, then respect for Market Forces is lost. A free enterprise system with human rights for each individual is essential for the success of any organization, thus the extraordinary success of the USA from 1776 to the present.

However, today, the prevailing undercurrent of thought in the media and in the universities is that enlightened values could create a society that would be far better and more utopian than those attempted earlier. It is often the case that the educated are the product of "groupthink" which is a closed system of thought that is a product of peer collaboration that neglects the perceptions, thoughts and feelings of the people. Only by accurate polling of the people can we avoid imposing another form of totalitarianism under the guise of "enlightenment."

Once again, we must caution against such a tendency. ONLY the intelligence of Market Forces -- which consists of the free expression of each individual -- works. ONLY MARKET FORCES!!!!!

No centralization of power works. Not even the most advanced artificial intelligence can work. NOTHING can replace the insight and value of the people. NOTHING!!!!!! History has proven that there is a natural tendency of people to want to find "a better way," to create a better system, to institute values and laws that would make life better for everyone. This tendency is just not productive, and in fact is massively unproductive and lethal. The irony of life and history is that removing imposed social dictates, no matter how noble, is when lives prosper in every way. History has shown there is more intelligence in the being of people who are a product of billions of years of development than the intelligence obtained by science, academia, and university study, which are comparatively in their infancy. Our advances are important, but they do not come close to usurping the brilliance of Nature.

Our best means of moving forward is to discover the will of We the People. We must see each individual as a resource of information, a source of wisdom that receives valuable information, not just from their five senses but also from their innate intuition. A person's wisdom comes from much more than TV, radio, newspapers, the internet, the media, academia, and other influencers. This true wisdom is the product of billions of years of intelligence that is incorporated into our bodies and minds, and THAT is the real source of power. This wisdom must be collected without biases, without labeling, and with an abandoned sense of inclusion and comprehensiveness, **but never against the will and protection of the individual.**

These suggestions point to the ultimate democratic reforms. However, this movement must be balanced by means of representation in government (thus the value of a Democratic Republic). But the representation is just that... representation of the will of We the People; not dominance and control by the powerful. Such a movement will remove the gridlock the U.S. is experiencing today and propel us into the future by realizing more fully the genius of our Founding Parents. It will be the source of amazing growth, freedom and wealth, the likes of which the world has never known, as it has been proven that employing the resources and resourcefulness of the masses is far more powerful than the will of a few in control. This movement toward democratization and away from any sort of centralized power is the only way any type of utopia will occur.

CHAPTER VIII.

Communicating the Desires of We the People

First we must lose the idea that voting once every few years is sufficient to run our Democratic Republic. There must be much more communication between the populous, which is the repository of wisdom, and those implementing the interests of the people. Additional communication can give the people a voice in all matters related to policy and spending. The officials we have elected have failed us in representing our interests and in formulating policy that benefits the people and the nation. A system that requires our elected representatives to follow more closely the will of We the People must be implemented.

One means of communication may be through the better use of Income Tax Returns. We all are supposed to file income tax returns each year. Simple adjustments can be made on the tax return forms to include polling information from the people. Currently, the tax return calculates the tax due by each filer, but it does not question the filer as to how their tax money is spent. We all know the "golden rule" -- he who has the gold makes the rules. Well it's time We the People made the rules.

As we discussed above there are twelve departmental agencies in government that comprise Discretionary Spending, plus additional departments that provide social programs that the people fund and the government disperses (Social Security, Medicare, Medicaid and other social programs) called Mandatory Spending. An additional page can be included at the end of the Income Tax Return that polls the Taxpayer regarding his/her interest in the amounts of tax money that are applied to each agency. There are sixteen agencies all together. All sixteen agencies can be listed with the percentages of tax dollars currently paid to each agency. Next to each line, one of three boxes can be checked to keep the same, increase or decrease the percentage of one's tax dollars applied to the respective agency. A fourth box can be included that allows the Taxpayer to write in the percentages of tax dollars that s/he wants applied to each agency, with the total having to be 100% of the total PROJECTED INCOME (not of the total budget). Three additional pieces of information must be included and listed IN RED: the amount of overspending from the prior year, the total amount of the National Debt and the interest we are paying on the National Debt.

This page may be called the "Taxpayer's Proposed Budget Form."

Giving all people this information related to their tax dollars accomplishes several things: It educates the people regarding how their tax dollars are spent; it educates people as to how much overspending is occurring; and it requires each Taxpayer to accept responsibility for the spending process, our deficit spending and our National Debt. This process would reduce the wrangling of politicians between branches, gridlock in Congress, the closing of government functions due to inaction and inability to compromise, and the resulting deficit spending. The results would be tallied by an independent organization and then presented to the public and to the elected officials who are required to fulfill the will of We the People. The people's voices would be heard and represented properly, and overspending and negative cash flow should be eliminated.

Overspending, deficits and debt are primarily the result of paying for Mandatory Spending related to Social Security, Medicare, Medicaid, Housing Assistance and some other Social programs, although there has been other emergency spending that have caused additional debt, such as natural, environmental and man-made disasters, funding for wars, and COVID-19 shutdown assistance. The Taxpayer's Proposed Budget Form should include a statement that for "every trillion dollars of national debt, the Taxpayer is ultimately responsible for payment of additional taxes at a rate of $1000/year for ten years."

Emergency funds should be incorporated into the overall spending plan so that emergencies do not cause additional debt. Spending should include the twelve agencies that are funded with Discretionary funds, the four agencies that include Mandatory Spending, and an additional line representing funding for emergency savings. The total of all funds proposed to be spent must not exceed the projected income for the same year. In other words, the government MUST balance its budget. And if there is any risk that the budget isn't balanced, then a Balanced Budget Amendment must be legislated.

Social Security must be corrected as reviewed earlier so that there is no more negative cash flow: all tax filers must contribute to the Social Security Fund at the current rates, and the fund should gradually be privatized beginning now. Additionally, as each working American builds their wealth with mandatory retirement savings, less and less social programs for housing, food and public assistance would be necessary. It will still be necessary, but far less than now.

Medicare and Medicaid must pay for themself and not be subject to cost overruns. As these two agencies are included in the list of departmental expenditures, then We the People become responsible for allotting amounts for these programs, thereby taking the decision-making out of the hands of politicians who are currently legislating medical treatment and coverages, while making promises to the American people (that often cannot be funded) in return for votes.

These principles are commonsense principles that are used by every family in the country to maintain their household and their businesses. The government should do the same! Additionally, we Americans must have a say in how our money is spent.

The citizens of this country are very upset with the overspending, the gridlock and overall lack of service of our lawmakers. The lawmakers are in a no-win situation that requires them to fulfill the interests of those that placed them in office while dealing with a larger body of legislatures that have diverse, conflicting and often opposing interests. The answer is to turn over the issues to We the People and let us decide.

As the system stands now, here is an example of how the Tax Payer's Proposed Budget Form might look, although I offer better examples in the following chapters:

Agency	2019 expenditure (billions)	Expenditure as a Percentage of Total Projected Income of $3.5 trillion in 2019	Check to keep same percentage	Check to increase percentage	Check to decrease percentage	Suggested percentage (total must equal 100%)
Agriculture, Rural Development, and Food and Drug Administration	23	0.66%				
Commerce, Justice, and Science	64.1	1.83%				
Defense	606.5	17.32%				
Energy and Water Development	44.6	1.27%				
Financial Services and General Government (includes Judicial Branch, the Executive Office of the President, and District of Columbia appropriations)	23.4	0.67%				
Homeland Security	49.4	1.41%				

Interior and Environment	35.6	1.02%					
Labor, Health and Human Services, and Education	178.1	5.09%					
Legislative Branch	4.8	0.14%					
Military Construction and Veterans Affairs	97.1	2.77%					
State and Foreign Operations	46.2	1.32%					
Transportation and Housing and Urban Development	71.1	2.03%					
Social Security Administration (yellow highlight)	1,041	29.74%					
Medicare (yellow highlight)	645	18.43%					
Medicaid (yellow highlight)	419	11.97%					

Supplemental Security Income, Housing Assistance, Other Programs (yellow highlight)	672	19.2%					
Emergency Funding	0	0%					
Amount of interest paid on Debt (red ink)	574 (red ink)	16.4% (red ink)					
Totals	4,400	131.27%					
Deficit (to be added to National Debt of $22 trillion in 2019 (red ink)	1,100 (red ink)	31.42% (red ink)	Not applicable	Not applicable	Not applicable	0	

Notes:

1. The 2019 Expenditures are per the Congressional Budget Office (www. CBO.gov, "status of appropriations, 2019"). The slight inaccuracies are due to variations in the CBO's published numbers.

2. The yellow highlighted agencies represent Mandatory Spending and by current law must be funded entirely.

3. This table reflects current law in funding the agencies of the US government. Suggestions to change the agencies or any part of an agency must be suggested through Polling Questions below.

4. Emergency funding is for budget overruns, funding for unplanned disasters, and other unexpected funding requirements.

5. (in bold red ink) **The National Debt has risen to over $25 trillion in 2020. It should be noted as a reference point that if $1000 in additional taxes were legislated to be paid by the average family in the U.S., it would take TEN YEARS to pay $1 trillion dollars; and increasing the corporate tax rate will increase the cost of products and services provided to the consumer.**

6. Next year's expenditures must equal or be less than the projected income so that zero dollars are added to the National Debt.

7. An additional 5.5% in emergency expenditures occurred in 2019 not allotted in the Agencies' 2019 Budget.

If you would like a referendum on any issue, please suggest a Polling Question below. All Polling Questions are tallied by an independent agency. When any topic has at least 10% of all Taxpayer's interest, a referendum will be presented to the citizens.

(Space for Polling Questions to be written)

A form similar to this one above can be submitted by each Income Taxpayer to suggest the manner in which the Taxpayer's tax dollars are spent.

The prior year's Expenditures are a reference point. The Taxpayer can accept the prior years' percentage, or request an increase or a decrease by checking the respective boxes. The Taxpayer can also indicate an alternate percentage thereby sending a message to lawmakers to spend according to the determinations of We the People.

As the system works now, there is no Emergency Fund for unexpected expenditures. An Emergency Funding category must be included in the budget, and should approximate the prior year's deficit spending, or a reasonable amount considering emergency spending in the past; possibly an average of the deficit spending for the previous five years.

As one studies the budget, it is obvious the predicament lawmakers have caused. Mandatory Spending comprises the majority of the budget (about 79%) and with the other necessary functions of the government, together cause a negative cash flow equal to 31% of total income. Therefore additional borrowing is required which in turn causes more debt and payment of more interest expense. We are in a vicious downward cycle that MUST be resolved.

Solutions to balancing the US Budget will be suggested later.

Another idea that would increase communication between the lawmakers and the people is the PROPER use of technology. Today we have such sophisticated technology that companies, governments and many agencies surveil nearly every action of the people constantly. We have the technology! We can use technology as a medium to communicate our interests to lawmakers and take back control of government, while incorporating protections and privacies that do not allow the information collected to be disseminated or used UNDER ANY CIRCUMSTANCES WHATSOEVER for any commercial or political partisan purposes, or any purpose other than the poll.

Here are just a few examples.

The Taxpayer's Proposed Budget Form which polls the spending of one's tax dollars referenced above could be submitted with one's tax return or it could be submitted online. Completing and submitting the Form via the web is advantageous as researching the US spending would be convenient while online. Websites related to spending by the government agencies can be searched at a few recommended sites such as the Congressional Budget Office (www.cbo.gov), US Spending (www.USAspending.gov) and Federal Spending Transparency (https://fedspendingtransparency.github.io/) quickly and easily all while the form is completed online. Simple, concise and efficient!

Traditional voting does not have to be eliminated. It's likely that some will use traditional methods of voting, but it's likely to gradually become less popular until it becomes entirely obsolete.

Many, many referendums as well as elections can be held online with assurances that the polling is accurate and that fraud is virtually impossible. Gridlock would all but disappear as issues would be settled very quickly by the electronic voice of the people. The polling process can be simple, concise, efficient, and inexpensive as compared to elections.

Single, double and triple means of identifying the voter can be instituted to ensure the accuracy of the vote and reduce the likelihood of fraud. Fingerprinting identification, facial recognition, iris recognition, video statements are just a few possible means of identification. Any combination of these methods plus additional technology along with acknowledged statements of authenticity under the threat of perjury can be used to submit votes and referenda when polling Americans.

Additionally, fail-safe protections must be instituted to protect the citizens from the collection and use of data for issues beyond the scope of the polls. Encryption, cyber vaults and multiple layers of security must protect citizens from dissemination of the collected data. Commercial enterprises would find the information invaluable. Political organizations could use the data to manipulate the citizens and affect policy. And the government can easily become a tyrant as it enforces values that "benefit the individual" or "benefit the greater good" at the expense of the individual's Human Rights. We the People must be able to communicate our positions on all matters relating to our governance without compromising our freedoms.

More specifics related to accurate identification and privacy concerns are discussed in detail in a later chapter.

We the People must decide on how our money is spent and on the issues of the day. The important matter is that We the People have control...NOT THE POLITICIANS, NOT THE CORPORATIONS, NOT THE WEALTHY, NOT THE LOBBYISTS, AND NOT ANY SPECIAL INTEREST. No centralized group of any description will take the power from us. The PEOPLE, as a collective, will have the power! The PEOPLE will make the decisions as to how to balance our national budget. The PEOPLE will decide on what new programs may be instituted and how we will fund them. The PEOPLE will decide if we want free tuition for universities in the U.S. The PEOPLE will decide if we want medical insurance for all Americans. The PEOPLE will decide if we want to change our economy to living on alternative energy and eliminating fossil fuels. The PEOPLE will decide if we want to have universal income for all citizens. Etcetera, etcetera, etcetera!

Every new idea proposed by any person or politician can be voted upon by the people at any time during the year. The idea can be presented in detail with references and qualified research material, along with the costs involved for the taxpayers. A detailed description of how each new program would be funded must be included in the poll along with any reduction in funding for other programs that may be impacted by the new program. The integrity of a balanced budget MUST be maintained.

This method of progress includes a holistic perspective. It includes a step-by-step means of moving forward, integrating existing realities, benefits, and shortcomings, with practical means for change. It eliminates great ideas and promises that cannot be funded, or cannot be funded without removal of other programs. It accepts the limitations of budgeting, and makes each citizen responsible for contributing to movements of the nation, the state, county, city, or the respective governmental polling jurisdiction.

This system incorporates the principles of democracy as envisioned by our Founding Parents. It eliminates the corruption that has infiltrated our system. It gives the power to the people so that We the People deploy government as the Founding Parents intended: Government of the people, by the people, and for the people!

It's the way our Founding Parents wanted it; it's what we have been charged to do, and it's the way to move forward as a nation, as a people, and as the human race. Disagreeing with this argument essentially disputes the premise of this treatise which is that history has proven that the most successful system of social organization is a free enterprise system founded upon human rights for all individuals, as evidenced by the last 244 years in the United States of America!

There will be extraordinary resistance to this movement to put the power in the hands of the people as it takes the power from those that have garnered it now. Politicians, power-brokers, the financiers, the ruling elite will fight to keep their power, money and the current system. The problem is that the current system is literally falling apart as the National Debt oppresses us with taxation, causing limited growth and progress, while threatening our national security; gridlock continues in government as highly financed politicians serve the interests of their supporters without compromise; the tendency toward centralization of seen and unseen powers threaten our dignity as human beings and our freedoms to express ourselves, worship as we wish and protect ourselves, harkening times when we lived under the rule of kings.

Granted, there is a risk in placing 100% control in the hands of the people. Pure democracy is not what the Founding Parents envisioned. Elected officials would continue to be the ones that make sense of the polls and implement the desires of We the People, and gradual transitions would be required. A Democratic Republic will continue to stand.

However, putting the power back in the hands of We the People resolves these problems elucidated above and greatly reduces the power of a centralized oligarchy to dictate behaviors. Transition to such a communication system between the people and the lawmakers is critical for our survival, and losing this battle will be the devastation of the United States and of the entire world.

If not for the United States of America, then who?!

CHAPTER IX.

The Purview of the Federal Government

We must identify what actually is the responsibility of the Federal Government as determined by the Constitution and resulting laws. Everything that is outside the purview of the Constitution that is managed by the Federal Government is a result of social programs that are funded by federal taxpayers' dollars. We the People must be completely aware of the social programs we pay for on a national level. And it must be remembered that any and all programs that do not have national consensus may be instituted on a State level, if the people of the State desire such.

The first objective of the Federal Government is to preserve itself, its people and its Constitution, which has as its foundation its adherence to Human Rights. Therefore, security is the government's number one priority. Since Human Rights and the autonomy of the individual are valued above strength and power, we are vulnerable to forces that seek to dominate, control and destroy our system and take our resources.

Fortunately the free enterprise system we employ facilitates the development of wealth beyond any other system of organization. The wealth that we have produced allows the research and development of the most advanced means of protecting ourselves through science and technology. **Our govern-**

ment must protect its free enterprise system which is the foundation of our security.

There are multiple issues related to protecting our free enterprise system.

<u>Private Property</u>. Private property is one of the basic tenants of a Free Enterprise System. Ownership of private property is an extension of the sovereignty of the individual as granted by our Constitution. Ownership of property carries with it a right to protect the property as well as accountability related to any harm one's property may cause. Infringement on one's Human Rights ultimately impacts one's property.

There are some that argue that our right to private property is corrupt; however, the alternative is not surrendering the property to nature. The alternative is surrendering the property to the government. The earliest of civilizations, tribes and peoples claimed and defended their territories. Such is the case today. The only two alternatives are allowing the individual to own private property or surrender property to a centralized authority. If freedom to own private property is infringed upon, then the people's Human Rights would be subjugated to the government. Therefore ownership of private property must be maintained and protected.

<u>Policy Issues</u>. Government programs and jobs must be limited. Creating government programs and jobs limits the means of problem solving, innovation, creativity and accountability characteristic of private companies.

Often, creation of government programs and jobs is the result of power plays by influential officials which may or may not be beneficial to the served community. Nevertheless, funding of each government program falls upon the Taxpayer.

As of June 2018, at least 2.8 million people are employed by the federal government (https://www.governing.com/gov-data/federal-employees-workforce-numbers-by-state.html) and an additional 1.65 million people still receive pensions from the US government (https://www.opm.gov/policy-data-oversight/data-analysis-documentation/federal-employment-reports/reports-publications/federal-civilian-employment/). An additional 14 million are employed by state and local governments (https://www.

statista.com/statistics/750777/number-of-state-and-local-government-employees-in-us-by-function/), totaling over 16 million people employed by all levels of government in the U.S.

The most current study available at this time shows that 20.2 million people are employed by federal, state and local governments in the U.S. which represents 14.5% of the total workforce (https://link.springer.com/chapter/10.1057/9781403920171_5).

There are positions that require government employed personnel such as members of the three branches of government, military personnel and other positions where service supersedes market forces; however, departments such as Department of Transportation, the Social Security Administration, Education, and other departments that could easily be privatized should not be part of the government. Government employed positions generally are not subject to market forces, consequently salaries are usually higher than comparable positions in the marketplace, benefits are better and pensions are often included. Most importantly, there is a general lack of accountability: cost overruns are common along with less than adequate performance, perpetuated by a pervasive attitude AT EVERY LEVEL **that funding is endless and fiscal responsibility is trivial**, which is absolutely delusional, antithetical to the marketplace and insulting to the taxpayer. Only after privatization of each government program and services are thoroughly explored and determined to be impossible should government run programs be allowed. Even after government programs and services are instituted, there should be a continued concerted effort to move each and every government program to the private sector.

Forcing the taxpayer to pay for programs is a variation of dictatorship, socialism and totalitarianism, even if the programs are noble in character. Enforcing such ideals is counterproductive to the interests and respect of the individual, human rights and the free enterprise system. This sort of centralized decision-making -- however limited it may be to any one or a few programs -- is counterproductive to progress. ONLY when people are given the freedom to innovate and problem-solve is wealth generated, as shown in the first 244 years of our free nation.

Socialized medicine is an example of limiting the incentives of innovation and the development of expertise for the benefit of lowering the price of services and making the services universal. The consequence chokes the growth of a vital industry, which in this case has lengthened human life on our planet, found cures and relief for injury and disease, and provided scientific knowledge that is making our lifestyles better every day. The same is true for education which has been smothered by government interference and would be greatly improved if the same funding was given to the private sector for education.

The most effective procedure to institute any new government program is by first establishing funding in the US Budget (with respect given to a balanced budget), and then by opening bidding to private companies who vie for the contract.

And again, it should be emphasized here that any programs that would be funded by the taxpayer is NOT a right. Rights are freedoms that are natural to people and codified into law to remove oppressions, and are not in any way costly to the people (i.e., are taxed), such as a right to free speech, press, worship and self-protection. There is no "right" to medical insurance for all, or other social programs that are framed as such. Such social programs are great ideas. If the taxpayers agree to fund such a program, then the program could be instituted through bidding to private companies with government oversight. And, if for whatever reason privatization is not possible, then implementation of the pre-funded program could occur through government management. But there is not a "right" or any sort of Human Right for a social program to exist.

Social programs exist only to the extent that the people agree to fund such programs with their tax dollars. Progress and wealth occurs in a cooperative environment; therefore, We the People must determine how much freedom we are willing to surrender as we adopt social programs that we want (not the politicians, not the lobbyist, nor any of the power-brokers).

Additionally, there are times when the government must support faltering manufacturers and services that are critical to the country and the economy. The government's role is to provide financing to such faltering organizations with soft repayment terms till restored or sold to alternative privately owned organizations, and never to take any type of permanent ownership of the organization.

The bottom line is that privatization is essential to the livelihood of We the People and of the wellbeing of the United States!

Abuses. Unfortunately there are some who look for ways to abuse the freedoms the U.S. provides. When free enterprise and freedom of thought, speech, press, worship, protection and the generation of wealth cause harm to others, then such behavior must be counterbalanced or, if necessary, regulated and penalized. Regulation should be a last resort as it must be balanced against the benefits of innovation. There also exists a responsibility of the individual to be reasonably aware of his/her engagements. Additionally there exists a responsibility on the part of the government to assess power centers that may abuse the people. Power centers that could potentially abuse the people are financial or corporate monopolies, racial dominant centers, ideological dominant centers, gender, religious, academic, technical and scientific dominant businesses and services, and any other exclusive group that seeks dominance in a sector that has the capacity to abuse the People. Such dominance must be identified and then counterbalanced.

The government can publish a list of businesses and services that it suggests would be beneficial to develop in particular areas, and can offer financing for such endeavors. Such a practice would allow the Market to naturally counterbalance power centers that have the capacity to abuse the people. Regulation would be necessary as a last resort if such counterbalancing efforts are not successful or until such efforts are successful. Again, it is the responsibility of government to facilitate the Free Enterprise System, not debilitate it. That means, taking an approach to build up rather than tear down.

Centralization of financial power. Competition must be fostered, even encouraged, in order to keep the economy vital. The government must study the economy in order to suggest and offer financing for beneficial areas of growth, as described above in "Abuses." If the government does its job in this area successfully, monopolies are not likely to develop as healthy competition balances supply and prices. Nevertheless, the government must limit the scope of any organization to dominate the economy or any sector of the economy.

Fiscal Responsibility. The government must balance its checkbook. It must not abuse the wealth of the system and the citizens by overspending, creating excessive debts or overtaxing its people. A Balanced Budget Amendment is necessary since the lawmakers have failed us in this area.

Contractual Enforcement. The government, through its Justice System, must oversee and enforce contracts so that the people and companies can rely on valid agreements, which are necessary to perpetuate the economy.

Government/Public Ownership and Government Employment must be limited. Government-owned organizations simply do not function as well as those in the private sector. The government must endeavor to privatize all government functions and only continue as public owned if and only if there are no alternatives. Accountability is limited in government organizations, thereby leaving opportunity for corruption, overspending, lack of performance and integrity, thus causing a drag on the economy; whereas private organizations must perform as contracted under the threat of losing the contract.

Certain functions are necessary to be performed by the government such as the representation of We the People, and the other functions listed in this chapter, but such services must be limited for the wellbeing of the economy and the Human Rights of We the People.

Facilitating Interstate and International Commerce. The government must institute systems that facilitate interstate and international commerce. Bidding for contracts must be sought to develop and maintain any and all means of commercial activity, such as all the transportation systems, postal services and electronic and high-tech media. Suggestions and recommendations with supportive financing should be offered to develop such systems by the private sector.

Resource Independence. The United States is vulnerable whenever we depend on other countries for essential products. An exhaustive inventory of our dependency upon products from non-democratic countries and then democratic countries must be made. The government then must recommend and offer financing to develop such products in the U.S. to reduce US vulner-abilities. Any and all laws, policies, regulations and treaties that interfere with this process of becoming self-reliant must be eliminated.

Our government must protect its citizens.

Security. Protection from harm from inside and outside our country is a primary responsibility of the government. Therefore, a strong military to protect the country from outside threats is essential; and law enforcement personnel at every level are necessary to guard against harm that may be inflicted upon the citizens.

It goes without question that the country must first define and protect its borders before the country can be secure, until there is absolutely no difference in political control, policies, and jurisdiction across borders, and We the People accept such. In other words, defined and protected borders are essential until annexation occurs.

You'll note that our Defense budget is $606.5 billion (as of 2019). Some say this budget is excessive and takes valuable money from the citizens of the United States. However, remember that a free enterprise system, a Demo-cratic Republic, can exist on its own; however a socialist or communist coun-try cannot. Socialist and communist countries must usurp market forces around the world in order to control world economies. They can continue to exist if and only if they take over the economies (and territories) of all other countries. The idea of a global command economy seems like it may harmonize the entire world; however, the premise of the Marxist System is faulty in that it disregards the inherent spirit of the individual to grow, excel, problem-solve and express oneself, which are all subjugated to the overriding interests of the State. Consequently, the United States MUST protect itself from the encroachment and insidious attacks as well as the violent attacks of despots and dictatorships. Such attacks include takeover of smaller nations by communist regimes, electoral interference, cyber-attacks, intellectual property confiscation, subsidizing manufacturing and employing child and slave labor in order to undercut world markets, and more. The U.S. must be on constant alert from powers that see our democratic approach with Human Rights at the forefront as weak and vulnerable.

As I see it, only a miracle worker could change the perspective of countries that value power first and maintain tyrannical views, but diligent efforts should be made by our country to negotiate peace, while we maintain strength and protection. If and when the threat is gone, then the $606.5 billion per year may be directed elsewhere.

The Safety Net. Many government services and social programs that assist the citizenry are not authorized by our Constitution and are secondary to preserving the Constitution and the security of our nation. In 2019, $361 billion was spent on combined programs that kept thirty-seven million people on "safety net programs" in the U.S. These programs include Earned Income Credit, Child Tax Credits, Supplemental Security Income programs for the elderly and disabled, housing assistance, school meals, child care, energy bill subsidies, and programs for abused and neglected children (https://www.cbpp.org/research/federal-budget/policy-basics-where-do-our-federal-tax-dollars-go).

The free enterprise system, though the most efficient and successful system in history, only works for people who are capable of operating within the system. An ability to make some sort of contribution is required to receive earnings and operate successfully in a free enterprise system.

We are living in a time where our country is existentially threatened by debt. We are attacked by external and internal attempts to dominate the people and our resources. And we are threatened by serious environmental dangers. **In order to survive, we must make use of all our resources.**

Most are capable of making some sort of contribution. If we remove our inhibitions and prejudices of the "disabled" and increase incentives and expectations for all to contribute, we can solve our problems. For example, Stephen Hawking, despite his debilitating disease, made extraordinary contributions to our planet and had a beautiful family. People with physical disabilities work in the private and public sector all the time earning income and self-respect. People with genetic and other mental challenges such as Down's Syndrome are making contributions and receiving financial and personal rewards. We must create conditions and incentives, along with implementation of practical schooling, training and apprenticeships, to encourage all to contribute. Nevertheless, there will always be a segment of the population that cannot earn enough to survive in a free enterprise system; therefore, a humanitarian safety net is essential.

As indicated earlier, one trillion, one hundred billion dollars ($1,100,000,000) were spent on medically related programs in 2019: Medicare, Medicaid, the Children's Health Insurance Program (CHIP) and subsidies related to the Affordable Care Act (ACA). Again, these programs are mostly funded by payroll taxes and the people's income taxes. Therefore these medical or insurance related programs are social programs in that they are funded by the people's tax dollars. These programs are by no means a "right" as many in Congress claim. They are tax-funded programs that the people fund and We the People must agree upon.

Medicare costs approximately $645 billion in 2019 as cited heretofore. Fifty percent was paid by means of income taxes, 35% by means of the payroll tax and 15% was paid by premiums (https://www.taxpolicycenter.org/taxvox/payroll-taxes-cover-about-third-medicare-costs)

The Medicare payroll tax is as follows: 1.45% of earnings are paid by the worker up to $125,000 in income if married, or $200,000 if single, then 2.35% over these thresholds; an additional 1.45% of the employee's earnings are paid by the employer with no earnings limitation.

Medicaid is entirely funded by federal and state income tax money. On the federal level, in 2019, taxpayers paid $419 billion, which was almost 12% of the total US government's income. The States matched the federal funding by means of the respective State's Income Taxes. Medicaid provides valuable health care benefits to low-income families including children, parents, pregnant women, seniors and people with disabilities. However, this is another social program that is entirely taxpayer funded and should be determined by We the People.

These social programs provide a significant benefit to our citizens; however, we will have to prioritize our resources in order to survive. We the People have elected lawmakers that have far overspent our current ability to pay for these programs and the result is a $25 trillion National Debt. Again, We the People must decide how we are going to spend our tax dollars and be fiscally responsible. We must FIRST decide how we are going to pay for or modify our current social programs BEFORE we can entertain additional expenditures. New programs such as Medicare or healthcare for all, housing for all, guaranteed minimum incomes for all, and other great ideas must be a) properly funded and b) properly implemented via means of the private sector with government oversight or by the government itself as a last resort.

Food Supply. The government also ensures that we have an adequate food supply. In fact we have been blessed with an abundant food supply, but there is significant effort necessary to protect the production and delivery of our food. The government provides measures to ensure that our food supply is healthy, nutritious and safe. The government is responsible for providing adequate and safe drinking water. It is also responsible for developing and maintaining the means for delivering products and services through transportation networks, while facilitating access to the energy we need to fuel our country's economy. These are essential services that provide the very basics of life's necessities.

Governance by Written Law. The government provides a Judicial System that is charged with applying the nation's laws equally and fairly to all, a Legislative Branch that makes the laws, and an Executive Branch that enforces the laws. Each branch is divided so the powers of the government provide checks and balances against the others. This system of counterbalances, along with a system of Rule by Law rather than rule by dictatorship prevents tyranny.

Social Advancements. The government also provides services that aid the people to develop as citizens that may in turn assist in the advancement of the country; therefore, the government provides labor supports, educational services, environmental protections and other services. These services are not necessarily required by Law or our Constitution, and must remain secondary to the security of the nation, but may be programs that We the People desire. Determination of such programs by politicians, corporations, lobbyists, the media or any organization other than We the People is against the Founding Parents' vision and the US Constitution. (A deeper discussion of our educational system will follow.)

<u>International Relations</u>. The government, specifically the Executive Branch with ratification by Congress, is responsible for international relations, including developing treaties, engaging in commercial activity, and dealing with threats and conflicts.

In summary, the responsibility of government is first the security and safety of the nation and our Constitution. These priorities must determine how our resources and tax dollars are primarily spent. Then additional services may be provided, as We the People decide and our elected officials implement, by agreeing to fund such programs. These services are the benefits of government that we receive as citizens and they induce an appreciation for the country We the People own.

CHAPTER X.

Taxpayers' Control of Spending

Yes… "own" … We the People OWN the US government. We the People are the Shareholders and the Decision-Makers of our government. Therefore, we are ultimately responsible for all its functions, thereby enjoying the benefits and enduring the failures of our government. We must take pride in our government, and we need to manage our government properly.

We can't just vote once every few years and expect that our voices will be heard. We can't just surrender to our elected officials all decisions that impact us. We must participate in the decision-making process. We must decide how our money is spent. And we must have a means to express our voice in ways that keep communication open and constant. We fall and rise with the health of this country, so we must be involved with its direction.

Earlier I suggested that an additional page could be added to one's Income Tax Return called the Taxpayer's Proposed Budget Form. The purpose of the form is to voice our concerns over how our tax dollars are spent. It is a simple form that could be completed quickly. It also has the proper information that will provoke additional thought, research and consideration by the Taxpayer. The form lists the twelve Appropriation Committees funded by government and the amount of money that was spent in each department the prior year. These twelve Committees determine "Discretionary

Spending". Also included in the form are four departments that are called "Mandatory Spending."

The next column indicates the percentage each department spent the prior year against the total income of the United States. It is NOT a percentage of the budget, as the government tends to create a budget that exceeds income by about $1 trillion dollars a year! The percentages listed are the amounts compared to the overall income of the U.S. So in order for us to control spending, we must look at each appropriation against the amount of money we collect instead of against the amount we budget. That is exactly what this form does.

Simple math allows the Taxpayer to see how much of their taxes paid are allotted to each department, and the Taxpayer can indicate in the following columns if s/he agrees with the percentage allotted the prior year, or believes the percentage should be increased or decreased. An additional column allows for suggested write-in percentages for each of the departments which all together must total 100% or less. Included in the list of appropriations is a row for Emergency Funding. This allocation should be equal to the deficit spending from the prior year, or at least the average of the deficit spending for the last five years.

The intent is to create a process that allows the Taxpayer to voice his/her opinion as to how his/her tax dollars are spent. An independent body must tally the results and present it to the public and to the lawmakers. More specific logistics are delineated in a later chapter.

This process would reduce the gridlock in Congress and alleviate many conflicts between the Executive Branch and Congress, while We the People take responsibility for governing ourselves.

But balancing income and expenditures will be more difficult than just this type of poll. In 2019, Mandatory Spending (Social Security, Medicare, Medicaid and additional social programs for the needy) amounted to over $2.77 trillion dollars and is over 79% of the income the U.S. received ($3.5 trillion), leaving about $730 billion to provide the essential services of government (Agriculture, Rural Development, Food & Drug Administration, Commerce, Justice, Science, Defense, Energy & Water, the Executive Branch,

Homeland Security, the Environment, Labor, Health & Human Services, Education, Congress, Military construction, Veteran Affairs, Foreign Operations, Transportation and Housing). The budget passed by Congress and signed into law by the President totaled $4.014 trillion, so that $1.244 trillion could fund these essential government services. But with cost overruns by various departments, emergency spending and interest payments on the National Debt, total expenditures amounted to over $4.4 trillion with total deficit spending of $1.1 trillion!

The deficit spending amounted to nearly the entire cost of providing essential government services!

So if we are to balance the budget -- AND WE MUST -- then we must make some decisions.

First, we MUST privatize as many programs as possible. The government has no business managing our pensions; it has done a poor job with education and has not maintained our transportation infrastructure. All three programs are extraordinarily expensive and fraught with cost overruns and low accountability, all of which contribute to deficits every year.

The Social Security Administration can be made solvent and quite successful immediately if the suggestions presented earlier to privatize are implemented. The payroll tax and employers' match should be instituted for ALL earners, not just the lower tiers, and the additional income obtained invested in the stock market to achieve an average of 5% per year. The funds should be saved for years 30-50 during the transition to privatization (as indicated in an earlier chapter, Transition to Privatizing Social Security). New earners would pay into their own pensions with safeguards and restrictions that are similar to IRAs, 401Ks, and other retirement accounts. Within fifty years, the county's pension plan (a privatized Social Security System) would be fantastically successful as the privatized funds are invested in the stock market, bonds, and notes compounded over 40-50 years. The average US worker would have over $1 million in equity which would probably be invested in the US economy; while at the same time, the US government is released from managing a department it has managed poorly and the taxpayer is relieved of additional taxes to save a poorly administered program.

Currently removing the Social Security Administration from the budgeting process would remove $100 billion from the deficit and later requirements to increase taxes. As defined, it would be its own department that is entirely self-sufficient.

Most of Medicare, all of Medicaid, and all additional support funding Supplemental Security are taxpayer-funded as cited earlier. Though they are Mandatory, we will have to find a way to pay for these programs and balance them with the twelve other departments of government. My suggestion is to reduce the portion of Social Security payroll taxes from 6.2% to 5% paid by the worker and the same matched by the employer (without any income caps) and then increase the Medicare tax to 2.65% for the worker, matched equally by the employer. The overall amount taxed would be the same (7.65% for the worker and the same for the employer) so to avoid tax increases. However, more money could be directed to Medicare as the Social Security Program is privatized, and income taxes would be less stressed.

Regardless what I believe, this conundrum of balancing the US Budget should be submitted to the American people. We must together decide where our tax dollars will be placed.

Also, over the years, the functions of each department have become confused and overlapped. Clear definitions of each department would make each department function better. Therefore, a revision of the departments should be something resembling this table with the current departments listed on the left and the propose departments listed on the right:

Agriculture, Rural Development, and Food and Drug Administration	Agriculture
Commerce, Justice, and Science	Commerce
Defense	Government Functions (Executive –including State and Foreign Affairs, Legislative, Judiciary)
Energy and Water Development	Energy
Financial Services and General Government (includes Judicial Branch, the Executive Office of the President, and District of Columbia appropriations)	Environment (Water Quality, Air Quality, Land, Forestry, National Parks, Interior)
Homeland Security	Defense and Homeland Security
Interior and Environment	Education (including Science and Technology development)
Labor, Health and Human Services, and Education	Labor

Legislative Branch	Health (including Food & Drug Administration)
Military Construction and Veterans Affairs	Health and Human Services (including SNAP, Housing, Supplemental Income, Medicare and Medicaid)
State and Foreign Operations	District of Columbia
Transportation and Housing and Urban Development	Transportation

The reorganization of the departments proposed above is just an example. The departments can be reorganized in another fashion, but the intent should be clear definitions for each department. And then each department might be subdivided into more specific sub-departments, all of which would need to be publicized so that the US citizens can determine what amount of their tax dollars will be directed to each agency. And, once again, the budget MUST be balanced so that income is at least equal to or more than the expenditures. Additionally, the expenditures must include an Emergency Fund for unexpected expenses that equals the average of the deficit from five years earlier.

With these proposed changes to the Departments in government, the Taxpayer's Proposed Budget Form, which may be applied to the end of the Income Tax Form, may resemble something like this table below.

This table uses variables to represent the allotments and percentages and is for the purposes of example only. The purpose is to show a) that the departments should be clarified and better defined, b) the Taxpayer must be able to see last year's total spending by each department, and c) the Taxpayer can communicate to the lawmakers to keep or to change the allotted percentages of each department. This endeavor is vital to remove the power from the oligarchical special interest groups, lobbyists, corporations, lawmakers and other power brokers, and place the power in the hands of We the People as the Founding Parents intended. Making such a transition and implementing this concept will more fully realize the principles of our founding charter, and allow us to grow as a Democratic Republic.

Department	Last year's spending ($billions) (includes Discretionary & Mandatory Spending)	Last year's percentage of TOTAL SPENDING (including borrowed money, if applicable)	Check to -Keep same PERCENTAGE -Increase PERCENTAGE -Decrease PERCENTAGE	Suggested Percentage Changes (must total 100%)
Agriculture	$A	z%	O Keep same O Increase O Decrease	
Commerce	$B	y%	O Keep same O Increase O Decrease	

Government Functions				
Executive, State & Foreign Affairs	$C	x%	O Keep same O Increase O Decrease	
Legislative	$D	w%	O Keep same O Increase O Decrease	
Judiciary	$E	v%	O Keep same O Increase O Decrease	
Energy	$F	u%	O Keep same O Increase O Decrease	

Environment			
Water Quality	$G	t%	O Keep same O Increase O Decrease
Air Quality	$H	s%	O Keep same O Increase O Decrease
Land	$I	r%	O Keep same O Increase O Decrease
Forestry	$J	q%	O Keep same O Increase O Decrease
National Parks	$K	p%	O Keep same O Increase O Decrease
Interior	$L	o%	O Keep same O Increase O Decrease

Defense International	$M	n%	O Keep same O Increase O Decrease	
National (Homeland)	$N	m%	O Keep same O Increase O Decrease	
Education Schools and Training	$O	l%	O Keep same O Increase O Decrease	
Research & Development including Science & Technology	$P	k%	O Keep same O Increase O Decrease	
Labor	$Q	j%	O Keep same O Increase O Decrease	
Health (including Food & Drug Administration)	$R	i%	O Keep same O Increase O Decrease	

<u>Human Services</u> SNAP	$S	h%	O Keep same O Increase O Decrease	
Housing	$T	g%	O Keep same O Increase O Decrease	
Supplemental Income	$U	f%	O Keep same O Increase O Decrease	
Medicare	$V	e%	O Keep same O Increase O Decrease	
Medicaid	$W	d%	O Keep same O Increase O Decrease	
<u>Transporta tion</u>	$X	c%	O Keep same O Increase O Decrease	

District of Columbia	$Y	b%	O Keep same O Increase O Decrease	
Emergenc y Fund	$Z	a%	O Keep same O Increase O Decrease	
Payment to National Debt (red ink)	$XX (red ink)	xx% (red ink)	O Keep same O Increase O Decrease	
Totals		100% of money spent prior year		100% of total income

Elected officials and their assisting bureaucrats will continue to play a vital role as the details of each department's expenditures will have to be managed. By no means would we become a pure democracy. We will remain a Democratic Republic; however, the expenditures and consequently the services of government will be managed according to the will of We the People, thereby manifesting more closely the vision of our Founding Parents, Lincoln and the great women and men that helped build this country.

This plan would reduce spending to the amount of money that is collected in total revenues; consequently, spending would decrease about 32% given 2019 numbers. The lawmakers would receive their budgets as determined by We the People and their duty is to find a way to provide ALL the services already provided within the limits of their budget. Essentially, each department, each of the lawmakers that oversee a department, and the bureaucrats that work within each department will seek private bids from the people in the U.S. to provide specific services within the terms of the budget allotted. Apprentices and interns should be utilized whenever possible as they are usually low cost and motivated. I GUARANTEE that each department will find competitive bids from a variety of companies and people to do the work with efficiency, excellence and accountability! If the contractor doesn't perform as contracted, then secondary or back-up bidders must be available. If the government personnel responsible for oversight fails or does poorly, then replacements must be made. If the lawmakers fail in their charge, then they must be replaced through elections. The bottom line is that government services must be provided within the constraints of the budget and in the amounts determined by We the People.

A few issues should be discussed regarding the Taxpayer's Proposed Budget Form.

Some fear that the Taxpayer may suggest allotting significant amounts to one program or another thereby reducing or eliminating other programs in government. For example, if 80% is allotted to Defense and defense-related functions, only 20% would be allotted to all the other departments, making each of the other departments small and ineffective. Or if 80% of the Taxpayers dollars are directed to social programs, then only 20% will be allotted to the other departments that provide essential government services.

To guard against this possibility, a limit of 10% change in any department should be instituted within a year. If the Taxpayer is intent on reducing or increasing funding the following year, the Taxpayer can suggest such, and departments can be progressively changed over time, but not drastically.

In such circumstances, it will be the role of the Elected Officials to present to the Taxpayer the benefits of each department and why the respective departments should be funded. Theoretically, such a lopsided movement would not develop since the taxpayer poll would come from all segments of the U.S., thereby balancing the overall percentages of each department. However, if polls determine that the people want to move in a particular direction, then the lawmakers would be obliged to follow.

Additionally, and most importantly, the massive financial incentives that lobbyists offer to our elected officials would be redirected from the lawmakers to the people. The real or implied indebtedness the lawmakers have to those that are currently financing their campaigns would be removed, and the lobbying organizations would then have to present their cases via the media to the people.

Current law mandates the funding of specific departments that are critical to the United States. So in the event that the US encounters a conflict between the taxpayers' determinations of funding certain departments against laws that must fund other critical government functions, then the law must prevail until changed. The People need to voice their will regarding such laws and would be enabled to do so through the proper means of polling, which is discussed at length later. Nevertheless, this Form requires the Taxpayer to be fiscally responsible and to direct the lawmakers to balance the budget. Since our elected officials have been overspending $1 trillion dollars a year, We the People must take control and do what the lawmakers have failed to do.

Balancing the budget will require a degree of austerity. We have overspent so much in the last twenty years that we are over $25 trillion in debt! We have no choice but to do what we must to live within our means, make better use of all our resources and privatize everywhere possible. Once again, I would suggest a maximum change of 10% per year in any department even as the overall US Budget is brought into balance. Consequently, a balanced budget could be achieved in about three years using the methods described above: privatization, a better use of resources and a 10% change in budgets per year.

A Balanced Budget Amendment would be essential. Such an amendment would be counter to the short-term interests of the people, the States, and the power brokers as all experience the immediate benefits from the over-spending of the federal government. However, the long term interests of our country are at stake. Again, it will take TEN YEARS for all the families in the U.S. paying an ADDITIONAL $1000/year in taxes to repay just ONE TRIL-LION DOLLARS IN DEBT! Currently, with a $25 trillion National Debt, we would be paying an EXTRA $1000/year for over 250 years. A Balanced Budget Amendment is a MUST so that we do not add to our debt!

Therefore, as a US citizen, a shareholder in the US government, and a decision-maker as ordained by our Founding Parents, I call for legislative action to enact a Balanced Budget Amendment in order to secure the interests of the United States and the interests of We the People, owners of this great country.

Some will say that reducing our spending on defense and defense-related matters will make us more vulnerable to the nations that are building their militaries and attacking the U.S. directly and indirectly. These concerns are valid and the U.S. must be protected from other countries that value power and control over freedom and Human Rights. All of history, except for the last 244 years, has progressed by means of one country conquering another and the victor enslaving the people of the defeated nation. The United States of America is the exception to this historical trend throughout all of civilization in that it values Human Rights above power and control of resources. Our democratic and Human Rights values have spread to allied countries, which is beneficial to the cause of freedom; however, all democratic countries will forever have to protect themselves from the onslaught of those countries that continue to value power over freedoms and who require conquest in order for their centrally-planned economies to survive.

Along with strong protections, the U.S. must engage more diligently than ever before to reconcile our differences with countries with centralized controls. Deep dialogue and education should be employed to enlighten the people and the leaders of despotic nations. Additionally, we must be open to learning and changing as we become enlightened to other's perspectives, while maintaining our fundamental principles of Human Rights. This effort is likely to be a massive undertaking, and a long term perspective is required;

but such an effort is essential for peaceful international relations as well as our own country's well-being.

For example, the Chinese have developed a 5G internet network that has significantly more capacity to transmit far more data much faster than 4G networks. However, this 5G network also has the capacity to surveil and collect the data of all information moving across its network. Consequently, the U.S. has determined that utilizing this Chinese-developed network would make our departments, institutions and agencies vulnerable to the Chinese. So, the U.S. is blocking the use of this Chinese network in US properties.

The Chinese believe such action is unwarranted and have considered retaliation against this US defense.

Conflicts like these present opportunities for intense dialogue. Although China is ruthlessly intent on taking over the entire world, and we have fundamental differences in perspectives, politics and economics, we are obligated to engage in negotiations to reconcile. The fact is that both countries will become similar albeit each from opposing positions if the current trajectories of each country is likely to continue. The U.S. with Human Rights and Free Enterprise is employing more social programs to act as a safety net for those that are disenfranchised and incapable of operating in a free enterprise system, while China is discovering that a free market approach is critical to growth and wealth, which may lead to freedoms for the Chinese people.

To reduce this idea to a simplistic explanation, negotiations related to the conflict of the Chinese 5G network might follow this approach: the Chinese network could be given access to the US market if the vulnerability of surveillance and confiscation of data was verifiably nullified. Then both parties would benefit. The US people could enjoy the benefits of a cutting-edge technology that competes with similar American made networks, while the Chinese have the opportunity to market their product in the U.S.

Maybe in the process, both parties will learn something. Maybe the Chinese would understand more fully our perceived threats to our freedoms and free enterprise foundation, while we discover more fully the benefits of a government subsidizing economic growth. Such dialogue that leads to the reconciliation of fundamentally different perspectives has short-term and long-term benefits that affect military conflict, political and economic relations, and the overall enrichment of cultures. Even if such an engagement is futile, even if the Chinese only continue to try to exploit our freedoms and vulnerabilities, even if negotiations repeatedly fail, we must continue to negotiate interminably. Hope must reign eternal. But we must be prepared for the alternative.

Another idea related to the spread of democratic values is to use technology to give people from other countries a voice in a similar fashion as proposed in the U.S. People from countries all over the world can be polled in an organized and official manner via the World Wide Web. As long as the privacy of those polled is protected, such information can be shared with countries that give no voice to their people, and constructive suggestions for growth and conflict resolution could be offered.

In summation, We the People are at a point in history where we are obligated to develop our Democratic Republic by more closely realizing the principles upon which we were built. We must be able to express our interests related to how our tax dollars are spent as well as all other issues of governance, while remaining alert to the threats of tyrannical countries that seek to confiscate our resources either directly by military means or indirectly by more insidious means.

CHAPTER XI.

Paying the National Debt

If We the People are to become financially strong once again, we will have to get our National Debt under control. I have discussed the means by which we can stop adding to our debt by privatizing many of our government functions, balancing the budget, and taking control back from the political power brokers, special interests and centralized policies. All these changes are important to stop deficit spending and to move us forward as a Democratic Republic. However, the National Debt still looms like an albatross that is over seven times our county's annual income, places an additional $83,000 of debt on every man, women and child in the U.S., and will take over 250 years to pay if every family in this country pays an additional $1000/year in taxes! The National Debt is a horrific burden caused by our elected officials that have spent about $1 trillion more each year than all US revenues for the last twenty years. Our lawmakers have failed us and are ruining this country! It's time we took the power back and rectified this terrible situation.

The U.S. has arbitrary limits on how much debt it will allow. The Debt Ceiling is raised by our lawmakers whenever a new problem arises or conflict within the political parties can't be resolved. Essentially there is no account-ability as each generation of lawmakers leave their mess for the next generation of taxpayers and lawmakers. The private sector, however, does have standards. Banks will lend no more than three times the borrower's annual income, provided the borrower has little to no other debt. This same standard should be applied to our National Debt. Currently, the U.S. has an income of about $3.5 trillion per year. Therefore, the maximum debt the U.S. should have is $10.5 trillion. We must make it a national priority to reduce the National Debt from $25 trillion to $10.5 trillion, a reduction of $14.5 trillion.

We can do it without raising taxes if we follow the suggestions outlined earlier in this book.

Social Security must be privatized. Directing the worker's tax and the employer's matching tax to a private fund without annual income limits owned by the worker and regulated like IRA and 401K accounts will develop into a large sum of money as regular contributions grow over many years of compounded reinvestment. Consequently, citizens are given an extraordinary incentive to work as opposed to seek benefits from social programs. The overall costs of social programs will go down. Citizens will develop equity that makes them "vested" in the U.S. as they own significant sums of money in their retirement accounts, and more investment is made in oneself, one's family, and one's community. Poverty will be reduced greatly and many of the negative consequences of poverty will be reduced in all communities, especially low income communities.

Commitment to the U.S. and patriotism will rise as crime rates will go down. Disincentives naturally develop to being out of the workforce, to being imprisoned, and to the potential loss of vested funds for committing felonies.

Not only will the taxpayer be relieved of the likelihood of bailing out a failing Social Security Administration, but the secondary costs related to low-income assistance for people, families, and the elderly will be mitigated significantly, overall costs to the US Budget will be entirely removed, and the SSA would become completely self-sufficient and extraordinarily productive.

Incentives must be given for ALL people to work, including the poor, disabled, and mentally challenged. Nearly all people can and inherently want to make a worthwhile contribution and should be incentivized to do so.

High school students should make contributions to companies and organizations through apprenticeships and internships, thereby creating a pool of labor that is free to very-low-cost in return for training in a career field. The taxpayer's costs of high school and college education will be reduced significantly, and production and services will increase dramatically.

Privatizing as many departments as possible such as transportation and education and the services within each department will reduce each department's costs significantly, with more savings realized over time if incentives are instituted. The private sector is always more efficient, creative, and accountable in comparison to the public sector. Performance and services will continue without interruption, with more efficiency. A diligent effort must be made to privatize as many government services as possible.

Each year as the Taxpayer completes his/her Income Tax Return, an additional page polls where the Taxpayer would like to have his/her tax dollars spent. This "Proposed Taxpayer US Budget Form" would require the Taxpayer to authorize what programs would be funded and in what amounts while balancing expenditures with income and eliminating deficit spending. A Balanced Budget Amendment is also required to ensure that no additional money is added to the National Debt and that We the People and the lawmakers are fiscally responsible.

If we follow these suggestions, we will reduce our spending significantly. We will be able to balance our budget. We will eliminate deficit spending. And we will be able pay about 10% of our income (which is currently about $350 billion dollars a year) to the National Debt. This pay-down would occur WITHOUT INCREASING TAXES! The balance on the debt will increase as a result of interest accumulation, but in about fifty years our National Debt would be reduced to $10.5 billion.

It's entirely possible to find additional income sources and funds to be directed to the National Debt. The current reserve fund of the Social Security Administration held by the Federal Reserve might be a source that could contribute to the Debt, as well as other funds and other means of income. Finding additional funding to apply to the National Debt is the commission of our brilliant economists and the charge of excellent leadership in our country.

We The People demand that the U.S. be fiscally responsible and reduce our National Debt to a reasonable amount, in line with standards in the private sector, if not to zero dollars!

CHAPTER XII.

Education

A few issues should be addressed regarding education in the U.S.

First, it must be acknowledged that the majority of people in the U.S. do not use much of the knowledge that they were force-fed in high school. Very few career positions require knowledge of Algebra II, Calculus I or II, advanced Literature, Biology, Chemistry, Physics, Art or Social Studies. The basics are essential, but advanced studies should be reserved for careers that require such study.

In contrast, most people DO need training in a) the use of Computers and Software Programs, b) basics in Financial Management (personal and business), c) Socialization Skills (such as respect for people of both genders, LBGTQ individuals, all races, ethnicities, and religions), d) education in Human Rights and their historical conflicts with centralization of power in politics and economies, and e) the skills involved with being self-sufficient and a contributing member of society (acquiring housing, food and medical care, as well as strong work ethic and entrepreneurship). These Life Skills are essential. They are more important than many of the advanced studies required in high schools and should replace such irrelevant courses.

When a student enters high school, s/he should begin an apprenticeship in a field of interest, and the study of advanced academics specific to the field. At least half of his/her time would be dedicated to the apprenticeship while the other half is directed toward the specific advanced academics of her/his chosen field and the Life Skills listed above. The student would engage in practical learning as well as in relevant academic study, without wasting the time and money of studying material that will not be used. In 2016-17, the U.S. on all levels of government combined spent over $739 billion on education (https://nces.ed.gov/fastfacts/display.asp?id=66).

Massive sums of property taxes are paid by home, land, and commercial owners to local municipalities and counties across the country for public education, and much of it is wasted. Additionally, in 2019, the federal government paid $81 billion for education across the U.S. (https://www2.ed.gov/about/overview/budget/tables.html, FY 2019 Congressional Action).

If such apprenticeship programs are implemented as suggested above, not only will the money that is paid toward schooling be used more efficiently, but the overall economy will experience the benefit of free to low-cost labor by young people that contribute to companies and organizations while learning a profession or a trade. Additionally, the development of practical skills will advance the career of the student while benefiting the community and the entire country in every conceivable area of life.

Changes in fields of apprenticeship would be possible; however, minimum standards would be required (i.e., two to four years) before apprenticeship is completed and the student-apprentice is eligible for hire. Continuing study and training for the student-apprentice could occur under the guidance of the teacher/master/employer in place of a liberal arts college education. Apprentices of all ages could engage in such training, allowing a means for people to change careers at any point in their work life.

Education has a foundational impact on all other areas of life. Refining our educational system, privatizing it, and making it more practical and responsive to the needs of children, families and communities will have an uplifting effect on all sectors of our economy, while increasing the quality of life for all people.

Currently, the standards that the U.S. dictates nationally are for the most part incongruent with the need to prepare our children for life and a career. Such is ALWAYS the case when centralized controls and dictates manage any program. Privatization resolves so many problems in this paradigm.

If the same money that is currently paid to the schools is offered to bidding individuals, companies and academic institutions that commit to specific performance and are overseen by government personnel on the national, state and local levels, then accountability and efficiency will be brought to education.

Private companies are unencumbered by generalized and outdated national standards that try to make "one size fit all." Private companies and organizations are more likely to be sensitive to the academic and training needs of children and the community. Ingenuity and innovation will be inserted into the K-12 curriculum which is lacking now. And everyone will benefit. The children will get the support needed to develop into contributing members of their community. The morale in schools will be instantly increased as the children can see a practical relationship between their studies, training, and their personal development. The extraordinary amount of wasted time suffered by the students, teachers and administrations will be changed to practical and productive time. And the massive amounts of money from local property taxes, state taxes, and federal taxes that are invested in our schools will be reduced significantly while providing a measurable return on our investment.

If the money that is paid by all levels of government was paid to the private development of schools from K-12, schools would naturally be more likely to implement a Life Skills Curriculum as well as apprenticeships due to the fact that private ownership is more in tune with the needs of those they serve; whereas the government, most often disconnected, is more likely to dictate generic values to the schools. Privatization of our educational system will greatly improve the quality of our schools and the achievement of our students, while reducing escalating costs and aligning the school system with the needs of the community.

Currently, the educational system from preschool through college seems to inculcate the student toward a lofty set of ideals that are not founded in practical applications. Aligning the education of the student with Life Skills and Practical Experiences will change the composure of our entire culture.

CHAPTER XIII.

Corporations and Organizations

Within our free enterprise system, we are free to develop any type of organization we can imagine as long as it does not engage in activity that is harmful to the people...people who are inside and outside of the organization. There are three components in all organizations: ownership, decision-making, and compensation. They can be set up in any manner the participants choose.

Many of the companies and organizations that have developed over the years are the result of well-financed individuals and organizations that focused all decision-making power in the hands of the owners. We call this "capitalism." Capitalism is just one means of organization within the Free Enterprise System. There are an infinite number of other means of engaging in Free Enterprising practices. "Capitalism" is not the economic system as commonly understood. "Free Enterprise" is the economic system, and capitalism is a description for one means of organization within the Free Enterprise System. The term "capitalism" has been misunderstood and has taken on incorrect implications, and as a result, the U.S., philosophers like Marx, and the entire world have treated capitalistic practices improperly.

Capitalism is a subset of Free Enterprise. Free Enterprise is a product of Freedom. Human Rights are natural freedoms that are codified into law and which feed the strength of the Free Enterprise System. Free Enterprise, in turn, reinforces the development and maintenance of Human Rights. It's a symbiotic, interdependent relationship.

Capitalism did not revolt against Feudalism as Marx wrote, but rather developed in an environment of freedom where Free Enterprise was the economic means.

Free enterprise has been in existence as long as humankind has been in existence. It began when one caveman traded his bear skin to another for bows and arrows, and it continues today as we shop for cell phones, trading our money for a phone with the features and price we prefer.

Capitalism refers to the practice of investing large sums of money (capital) to create a business that the common person or other groups cannot replicate. Consequently, the capitalist had leverage to control all decisions related to the business which usually benefited those that invested the capital.

As a result, the US government formulated rules, policies and laws that protect the workers. Unions developed to counterbalance the power of management. The overall result is that competing interests divide people within the same organization.

The proper role of government in a free enterprise system is to nurture competition. Protecting the free enterprise system is the government's first financial priority as the country's wealth finances the security, the sustenance, and the health of the people.

Facilitating the protection of the worker and the labor force has been important in the history of the U.S.; however, facilitating competition is just as, if not more important, and it has been for the most part neglected.

The U.S. should regularly study the economic impact of corporations in the U.S. and distinguish which companies have excessive advantage over others, whether in production, in pricing, in the treatment of its workers, or any excessive criteria. The instinct of politicians is to regulate against injustices and imbalances. A perfect example is the 400% increase in the price of the EpiPen. The immediate reaction of lawmakers after outcries from the people who were mortally dependent on the treatment was to lower the price of the treatment by law. However, such legislation would not have been necessary if the government was proactive in its duties. The government should have determined the vulnerability before the corporation took advantage of the people. The government's role is to encourage healthy competition so dominance in any field does not lead to abuses. Therefore the government may offer financing opportunities for individuals or organizations who were qualified to compete with the exclusive maker of the EpiPen before the maker could engage in abusive practices. Competition is a natural regulator that is a hallmark of the free enterprise system, and it is the DUTY of government to foster free enterprise.

Regulation, on the other hand, removes the incentive for competition. As in this example, no other companies are likely to seek to develop a competing EpiPen if the return on the investment is too low as a result of regulation. Consequently, the entire world loses.

Regulation as multiplied by each sector of the economy, by every industry, and in every business is an oppression placed upon the people and the free enterprise system, while fostering competition is an endeavor that promotes abundance for the people and the economy.

This overview is just a statement of the values We the People as the governing body must employ. It is not an implacable rule. Regulation is in fact necessary to protect the people in certain circumstances; however, it must always be limited in the interest of freedom, Human Rights and Free Enterprise.

Alternatives to companies that form unions and divisive entities within an organization can be developed that align the interests of the participants. There are many examples of such alternatives. Some companies make the workers in the organization shareholders and determine decision-making authority. Some companies include profit sharing. Others offer income-sharing percentages, where it's pre-established that workers share X% of the income, management receive Y% and shareholders Z%, or something of the kind. In such a pre-arrangement, all participants in the organization commit to the mutual interests of the entire organization, rather than creating divisive and opposing conflicts. As soon as the government steps in and determines how the internal relationships of the organization are to be implemented, divisiveness is institutionalized and the creativity of free enterprise is destroyed.

The government would serve the interests of the people by publishing suggestions for better organized companies and offering financing to qualified people and organizations that can develop superior or alternative-run organizations. If necessary, the government could implement limited and short term regulations till it fulfills its objective to foster healthy competition, rather than permanently legislating and centralizing decision-making in the economy.

Free enterprise will always reign supreme unless command economies overtake democracies. And, God forbid, if command economies do take over all democratic countries, given the billions of people on the planet and the multitude of organizations across the globe, it would be impossible to limit one from trading his "bear skin for bow and arrows" somewhere in the world. Free enterprise is a force of nature. Small business is one of the great solutions to poverty. It has been around since the beginning and will continue as long as humankind! Centralized economies and governments can only survive if they overtake the free world, and then still cannot sustain over time.

People, organizations, and the powerful who seek to control freedom of thought (however unconventional it may be), control freedom of expression (however inadequate if may be), control freedom of worship (however odd it may appear to be), and/or control freedom to protect oneself (however dangerous that may be), are architects of a global totalitarian order that is directly in conflict with the freedom and dignity of the individual. Again, regulation is necessary in some circumstances to protect the people from harm; however, such regulation must be secondary, temporary, and limited to the long-term interests of upholding Human Rights. We the People will decide together, regardless of our inadequacies, our mistakes, and according to the prevailing winds of time.

The US government must be proactive in researching products and services offered in the U.S. and determine where there are potential imbalances or domination by any business. If there is not enough competition for a particular product or service, the likelihood is that the business providing the product or service will begin to take advantage of the consumer. The government does not have to split up the business or regulate it, especially if the imbalance is discovered early. Rather, the government can offer opportunities for low-interest financing for new startups in the fields that need additional competition.

The government can provide information and make suggestions on a public website or in publications that offer opportunities with descriptions related to the government's reason for their offers, but do no more. The government is not responsible for running or controlling any companies or programs in the private sector.

Similar opportunities can be offered for businesses that promise better labor conditions, or hiring quotas, or any other criteria that counterbalances power. Making these opportunities available is far better than instituting laws and regulations that institutionalize disparities and are oppressive to the general economy.

Additionally, the government should study products and services purchased from other countries that the U.S. is dependent upon and include opportunities for US companies to develop replacements. First products and services purchased from centralized, non-democratic countries should be replaced, then products and services from other democratic countries.

There will be logistical problems related to the transition to self-reliance. Pricing may become a problem as lower priced products are sold from China and elsewhere. Temporary subsidies and tariffs to protect the new startups may be instituted for a limited amount of time. Also there are a multitude of parts that come from different countries that are incorporated into the manufacturing of a complex product like an automobile or a computer. Developing such complex products entirely or mostly in the U.S. may become a logistical problem. The bottom line is that the government is obligated to resolve such issues in order to secure the US citizens.

CHAPTER XIV.

Polling the Citizenry

In order for We the People to govern, we must make our voice heard by the lawmakers and bureaucrats. Voting once every few years simply is not sufficient. Currently politicians use informal focus groups to get the pulse of the people on a variety of topics. Polls are conducted by various organizations to do the same. However, a formal process of regular communication between We the People and the Lawmakers must be developed and instituted.

For example, a specific, limited question can be placed on a polling website for citizens to answer. The citizens would login and verify themselves with precautions which could be instituted through the use of identifying technology that would prevent fraud and abuse of the One-Person One-Vote standard (discussed in more detail later). The citizen would answer a clear and limited question or questions. The answers would be tabulated by an independent organization and presented to the public and to the lawmakers. The lawmakers are then obligated to follow the will of the people.

We have the technology to create such a process and create it with security and privacy. We also have the technology to ensure the certainty of One-Person, One-Vote. The system just has to be instituted, and it must be instituted for the sake of our Democratic Republic. Neither party affiliation nor the profile of the citizen should be included in the polling questions as that information only creates biases, antagonizes prejudices and exacerbates partialities.

Demographic information should be limited or eliminated in order to protect against labeling. The decisions of We the People should supersede profiling, identity politics, and demographics. The polling process would be as rigorous as a scientific study and should be regular, constant and pervasive. News organizations should be highlighting the current polling questions daily. Media, universities and relevant organizations should be discussing the pros and cons of each polling question. Answers to the polling questions would be required within a limited window of time, i.e., thirty days.

There will be a percentage of people who will not participate in the polling process just as there are a number who do not vote. However, making the polling process accessible to (but not required by) all people may bring more people into the process. Additionally, all that protest and express frustration with current policy have an avenue to directly express their viewpoint. This process follows the mandate of our founding charter.

As long as we utilize technology that protects the individual's right to privacy and security, the largest resistance to implementing such a process would be those that will lose their power such as the lawmakers, power brokers, corporations, and lobbyists. The playing field immediately becomes flattened. The poorest citizen will have the same power as any multi-billionaire. Every minority citizen has the same equal power to affect policy as the most connected power broker. The disadvantaged, the forgotten and the disenfranchised all would have the same equal voice in our government policies and spending as the oligarchical elite. That is the vision of our Founding Parents. Now in the twenty first century we have the means to realize this vision.

We the People claim the power that has been given to us in the US Constitution! We demand a voice in government! We demand to be in control of our policy! We demand to determine where our tax dollars are spent! We demand a pervasive polling process that allows each citizen a means to participate in governing!

Settling questions related to any new social programs can be made by the people. If We the People want to institute a social or government program, credible information related to the Taxpayer's costs and benefits would be included in the polling question. The costs must include the source of funding whether from the taxpayer or from other government funded programs. But with ANY new program, sacrifice is necessary and the costs MUST be weighed by the taxpayer. If the taxpayer/citizen votes an increase in taxes in favor of a new program, then that is representative of the will of the people, and it can be instituted by the lawmakers. If the taxpayer/citizen denies the program, then that is the will of the people and the lawmakers must follow. Such is the vision of the Founding Parents. Such is the solution to our gridlock in Congress and all levels of government. Such is the solution to the sense of betrayal and powerlessness that the US citizen feels. Such is the solution that will lead us into remarkable growth and development for centuries to come. Such is the process that will keep the United States the "City on a Hill."

The governmental structure as envisioned by the Founding Parents would not change. We would remain a Democratic Republic and our elected officials will continue to perform the duties of government, and lead the country in times of crisis. However, the incentive for special interests groups, lobbyists, corporations, the media and other organizations that funnel billions of dollars into campaigns and support politicians, and the incentive of politicians who prance around the country pandering to the people, offering new programs in return for votes, would be all but extinguished.

CHAPTER XV.

Polling Logistics, Results and Implementation

Each citizen would register approximately two months prior to being eligible to vote or engage in polls. Registration would occur by means of setting up an account that included personal identifying characteristics that could be collected via highly technical means. As an example, registration might include submitting one's fingerprint, picture of one's face for facial recognition, a voice sample for voice recognition, a picture of both of one's irises, a video of oneself, one's social security number, one's email, telephone number and a strong password. The information would be collected and stored in several layers of secure cyber vaults by the US government. Logins would require all means of identification in order to vote or participate in polls.

Polls can be conducted on each level of government: national, state, county, and city. A majority would naturally rule in the city, county and state polls and the lawmakers in each area would enact the laws based on the polling results similar to the current prevailing law. However, on the national level, the sovereignty of the States must be considered. Therefore, a similar concept as the Electoral College would prevail in national polls. A majority decision would be determined in each State. A representative from each State would vote in the National Poll based on the position of the State. The results from a majority of the States would determine the outcome. Lawmakers would then write and institute the laws just as it's done now between the two Chambers of Congress with approval by the President; however, the entire process is enacted with a fiduciary effort to fulfill the will of We the People as expressed in the poll results. The legislative process would be similar to our current system but without the wrangling of politicians who are influenced by loads of special interest money. Such a system would preserve the culture of each region in the U.S. while allowing all the respective States to present the voices of their people on a national level.

One note related to establishing voting districts: If the will of We the People is to be followed as closely as possible, then the drawing and redrawing of voting districts should be eliminated. Voting districts should follow a non-biased grid pattern placed over each state, or some other geometric pattern that is drawn without any partiality. Such an impartial system is the only way the political melting pot of the U.S. can be realized, whereas the practice of gerrymandering perpetuates differentiation and partialities, further dividing the people.

Polling questions can be presented as often as reasonable. If one issue was decided each month on each level, then twelve issues a year would be decided on each level of government all over the country. If more polls could be implemented without compromising the results, then more can be done.

Each polling question must be simple, clear, and limited in scope. Costs to the taxpayer related to the implementation of the poll question must be included such as the elimination or reduction of other government programs currently financed by the taxpayer, an increase or decrease in taxes, and any and all financial, social, and environmental implications would be included in a simple clear manner. The groups that advocate for the outcomes of issues would be able to present their position in the media during the Consideration Phase (i.e., thirty days), and the actual poll would allow a time period for casting a vote (i.e., thirty days). The results would be made public quickly (no more than thirty days) and the lawmakers would be required to fulfill the will of the people with temperance, moderation, and the 10% rule (the financing of social programs can be altered up to ten percent per year).

Theoretically, some states and communities would move toward less regulation, less government, and less taxation, and other areas may increase social programs, healthcare, environmental regulation, communal sharing of resources (i.e., taxation), and removal of private property, while there would likely be combinations of such programs in many other places. Such is the beautiful tapestry of our country. This system would allow people of like mind and culture to determine their destiny regionally, within the context of a national umbrella which provides services necessary to the whole. Although it should be noted that the US Constitution and our Foundational Principles of Human Rights and Free Enterprise would have to prevail on all national matters.

CHAPTER XVI.

Resistance from Those in Power

It should be acknowledged that extraordinary resistance is likely to occur on many levels.

The will of the people is directly contrary to the interests of those that endeavor to homogenize, centralize and control the people. These competing powers come from several sources.

Last year, forty-three special interest organizations spent hundreds of millions of dollars to influence lawmakers. Each of the forty-three organizations had at least three former lawmakers acting as lobbyists on the organizations' behalf (https://www.opensecrets.org/news/2011/05/big-companies-special-interests-hire-private-congressional-delegations-to-lobby/). The extraordinary amount of money in the lobbying industry and its impact is directly threatened by moving the power to We the People.

The fossil fuel industry receives billions in subsidies from the US government. The auto industry, housing, and healthcare receive billions also. Lobbyists are constantly advocating for these industries.

Powerful and wealthy political and corporate people seek to consolidate and increase their own power without the consideration and, most often, in direct defiance of the will of We the People. The consolidation and use of media outlets to manipulate the information and national dialogue is most disturbing. There are only five organizations that control most of all the media in the U.S.: AT&T, Comcast, Walt Disney, Viacom and Fox. Each is financed by advertising dollars, primarily from large national and multinational corporations, and each has their specific ideology and agenda, none of which seeks the interests of We the People. Rather, each seeks to perpetuate their corporate interests at the expense of We the People. The same is the case for public radio and television which has become subservient to the interests of their large donors.

In fact, ratings are highest and the media profits the most when the largest catastrophes, man-made and natural, are covered. These organizations directly influence lawmakers and the people in order to advance their interests which are often in direct conflict with the interests, inherent intelligence, and instinct of the people. The government is responsible for maintaining free enterprise in the economy by supporting competition in each field; however, our lawmakers have failed us once again as they have not made any effort to counterbalance the manipulated media, suggesting that they are complicit in the manipulation.

Providing a vision for the future is one of the benefits our elected officials can offer We the People. Every attempt to improve upon our condition should be discussed and studied. However, lawmakers regularly and unabashedly advocate for government programs that require compliance from all taxpayers. If the taxpayer understood the additional tax burden making public colleges "free" ($79 billion/year) (https://www.nytimes.com/2019/07/19/business/tuition-free-college.html#:~:text=But%20free%20college%20isn%E2%80%99t,need%20to%20foot%20the%20bill) or making healthcare "free" ($2.8-3.2 trillion/year) (https://www.crfb.org/blogs/how-much-will-medicare-all-cost), or eliminating fossil fuel energy ($4.7 trillion) (https://www.reuters.com/article/us-usa-carbon-report/weaning-u-s-power-sector-off-fossil-fuels-would-cost-4-7-trillion-study-idUSKCN1TS0GX), the Taxpayer may not comply. However, if it is shown to the taxpayer that such programs may actually save the taxpayer money and/or convince us that the investments are worth our additional tax dollars, and if the programs can be accomplished within the realities of a balanced budget, then such programs should be instituted. Once again, We the People must decide, and we can make these decisions collectively if an official means of regularly polling the interests of the people is instituted.

Elections once every few years are not sufficient, and the contrary efforts of special interests, corporations, and desperate, greedy, pandering politicians are often in direct conflict with the interests of We the People.

Political campaigns receive billions of dollars a year from Political Action Committees, wealthy individual donors, and foreign sources. The media, national and multinational corporations, the intellectual elite, and all the other oligarchical power brokers all have a vested interest in maintaining their power and will use all their resources to keep their power over the people. The politicians are likely to be complicit as they protect their income sources outside of their government salaries. Experienced lawmakers and elected officials are not the problem, it's the money that diverts their interests and loyalties away from the people who have elected them, and it should be legislatively removed.

Change is best accomplished gradually and without violence. Once again, we have the best system in the world now, and we have made extraordinary advances in every area of life. However, we are at a crossroad that is requiring us to choose the path we will follow. **Currently factions -- each with reinforcing ideologies and financial support -- battle to maintain and develop their status, creating bulwarks and institutions, which are continuing to move the country in the direction of massive overspending, centralization of power, and the insidious loss of our Human Rights.**

Should we be limited to and pigeonholed into a two party system? Do we really need media outlets spreading their ideologies? Do we need our politicians deciding how our money is spent?

What We the People NEED is a means to voice our interests, and representation in government that fulfills our desires. That's what We the People need!

One last comment on government of the people, by the people and for the people…There is an irrational fear that if the people were in control, the government and the country would descend into chaos; and that the people would vote themselves excessive income, excessive benefits, remove all regulation, laws, and basic societal controls causing a downward spiral into oblivion. This fear is simply not warranted.

Human Nature has a hierarchy of needs that seeks safety, shelter and security as priorities thereby motivating the people toward the same protective systems that we have in place now. So, it is certain that police, fire and medical first responders will not be eliminated. Homeland Security and National Defense will not be eliminated. In fact, little to none of the current departments and programs currently in place will be eliminated, and the social structures will mostly remain the same. Our Democratic Republic will not be threatened in the least as all elected and government officials will continue to perform the duties of government as mandated by the Constitution. Most importantly, our elected officials will lead in times of crisis.

Each individual that participates in the polling process will act as an equal counterbalance against each other, so that no one person or group can dominate another, while we all together contribute to a collective will. States would keep their own sovereignty, representation and governments -- each with their own policies, laws and cultures. The Electoral College would remain to equalize the voice of each State. And overall, government on all levels would remain the same. The difference is that We the People will govern. We determine where our tax dollars are spent. We determine policies. And the elected and their assistants serve the interests of the people.

It is unrealistic to believe this polling process would determine all policy matters. After the system is refined, it's likely that six to twelve matters might be polled each year. More might be possible, but it is more important that the people engage in the decision-making process of the most significant policies. Eventually all important matters can be rendered to polling and We the People can decide on the overall direction of our country, but our elected officials will continue to guide the country on all other immediate government matters.

CHAPTER XVII.

Political Parties

In such a context where We the People determine policy, spending, and ultimately, our destiny, there would be no need for a two party system. The direction at each level of government is determined by the People with regard to each issue polled. Consistencies will naturally develop and the media and other institutions will be inclined to label such groups or movements, but the descriptions will be less likely to be broadly defined, party-like groups. Groups will most likely coalesce around a policy or an issue.

Additionally, since the polling process will incorporate protections against collecting demographic information, historical polling results, and any other descriptions that generalize populations, identity politics and institutional biases would be discouraged and may be entirely eliminated. The dissemination of any collected personal information would be strictly prohibited. A multitude of groups that represent particular issues would naturally develop and present their visions to the People relative to any particular polling question, and We the People would voice our desires without the institutional limitations of Party affiliation, political encumbrances, or privacy concerns. The two party system would become obsolete and is likely to evolve into a system that supports a multitude of groups, each of which represent relevant policy positions.

CHAPTER XVIII.

Protecting our Precious Planet

Environmental threats are ultimately the most dangerous of all. Polluting our seas, our air, our lakes, rivers and streams, our land, our skies, and any part of our environment is a violation and crime against our precious and rare planet, wildlife and all of Humankind. Every person, organization, corporation, and government must commit to leaving any place they visit or interact with BETTER than they found it.

Issues related to the destruction of our lands, waters, air and wildlife must be presented to We the People for remedy along with the costs of remediation and proper replacement. If the people become concerned about environmental matters and understand the costs -- environmental and monetary -- they are most likely to act, agree to programs and lead our lawmakers to action.

But action cannot and will not occur without the will of the People.

International agreements must be developed by all nations as these issues are global in nature.

The gravest threat to our planet is not fossil fuels, but rather nuclear fission fuels. As mentioned earlier in this book, there are ninety-eight operating nuclear power plants in the U.S. today, and 440 in the world, plus over 200 floating nuclear plants on our oceans. And there are approximately 75,000 nuclear fuel rods **in each plant.** (https://world-nuclear.org/information-library/nuclear-fuel-cycle/nuclear-power-reactors/nuclear-power-reactors.aspx) Each of the fuel rods last for about eighteen months and then must be removed from the plant and stored for at least 10,000 years while they remain dangerously radioactive.

We are creating a planet that is destined to burn up because of our dependence on nuclear fission.

We must develop technology that will counter the destructive effects of fossil fuels and nuclear fission fuels. We can clean the air, clean our waters, and clean our skies and our land if we commit to developing the technology to propel our world while keeping our environment clean. We CAN develop alternative fuels that are safe for us and for generations that follow.

Nuclear fusion may help as it appears to be safer, while causing a zero carbon footprint (https://phys.org/news/2012-10-safer-efficient-fusion-generated-electricity-horizon.html), The initial reaction of governments all over the world is to regulate and legislate when crises occur.

Again, it MUST BE EMPHASIZED that such regulation and legislation have to be made temporary and limited in order to maintain the sovereignty of Human Rights and preserve Free Enterprise. Of course, there must be a balance between Human Rights and the survival of the collective. The balance occurs when We the People decide how much freedom we are willing to surrender in order to resolve collective issues. But WE THE PEOPLE DECIDE! Not the government. Not the politicians. Not the environmentalists or any special interests. Not any of the power brokers in the oligarchy. The politicians, special interests groups, and all concerned can publicize their concerns, present their information and promote their positions in the media, and then We the People can decide to live and die by our own decisions, as tempered by, but not controlled by, our elected officials. That is how the Founding Parents envisioned our country and such is the means we have employed for the most part of the last 244 years which has produced the most successfully run organization in history, while maintaining our foundation of freedom.

If these issues are presented to the people in a poll with the appropriate pros and cons presented by representatives of all concerned, along with the costs to the taxpayer, the inherent intelligence of people can decide and the will of the people will prevail. Such movements of the people -- not only in the U.S. but around the world -- have been the most powerful social force on the planet!

CHAPTER XIX.

Into the 21st Century

After staving off the tyrannical onslaughts from the Japanese Empire and Nazi Germany, as well as the despair of the Great Depression, the culture in the U.S. was one of invincibility. The family unit was the central force which led to the expansion of home ownership and the spread of suburbia. The social consciousness in the U.S. had a sense that we, the U.S., together could overcome all obstacles and that peace between nations could develop. Then the Pill changed everything!

The development of the birth control pill led to a change in social values from a rigid sense of virtuous character to a permissiveness that allowed for sexual activity without consequence. The introduction of estrogen (female hormones) into the food supply reinforced the change in social consciousness, as did Hollywood's depiction of provocative and illusory women. Recreational drugs exacerbated this movement.

The culture changed from a paternal set of values to a maternal set of values within a generation. Consensual decision-making replaced authoritarianism in the home and in our institutions, and a generation of children was reared with a sense of egalitarianism and permissiveness.

We developed "earth consciousness" as we gazed upon the first images of the earth rising over the moon's horizon and the global Environmental

Movement was launched. The art in the culture reflected these changes as music placed women and feminine values as the ideal. John Lennon glorified an attraction to women in his songs as he sought the feminine approval missing in his childhood. We were encouraged to "Imagine" a world of peace without the debilitating influences of politics, religion, and economy. Theater changed from themes of the superhero that saved humankind from evil forces intent on taking over the world to minions who followed the most evil leader they could find.

The US government experienced the threat of Marxism as the Soviet Union became the leading proponent, along with Communist China, of a world order that included a shared economy, the removal of religion and a social structure that required the people to be subservient to the dictates of the State, while killing somewhere between 60-110 million people as they imposed their totalitarian, socialist policies on their people, and while threatening the world with their expansionism. Again, as described earlier, the only way such a system can survive is by means of complete world dominance eradicating the Free Market and Human Rights and replacing them with a Command Economy that dictates to subservient people their activity, expressions and values. The U.S. was in the precarious position of having to stop the advancement of communism while trying to appease the changing American culture. US policy--foreign and domestic--necessarily became more clandestine and the youth culture reacted with violence, riots and unrest till four Kent State college students were killed by our National Guard.

An entire American generation grew up with images of horrible assassinations. And a deep distrust of the US government was etched into our consciousness. Consequently, this generation became determined to implement the maternal values of the 1960s and 70s as they entered politics, education, media, and the universities.

Today we are experiencing the effects of these events from sixty to seventy years ago.

Authoritarian figures are perceived as fascist as they conflict with consensual values. Political structures are perceived as impediments rather than as a means for inclusion, order, and change. Religion is dismissed as a set of archaic regulations that are counter to science and modernity. And the values of a work ethic that earns comforts, status and wealth flies in the face of a culture where parents continue to support their adult children, privileges for minorities and the poor are institutionalized. and overspending and over indulgence becomes the norm.

Our children were guided through a school system and, for the most part, a liberal arts education that teaches idyllic values that conflict with practicality while being left with tens of thousands of dollars of debt and a sense that opportunity is limited to a fortunate few. Therefore many are unable to buy a home, marry, and have children as they are immersed in a system that does not serve their needs.

The prevailing political solution to quell the angst of this generation is to provide more and more government programs and services laden with politically correct regulations to the point where we expect the continuation of the massive government spending which exceeds a trillion dollars a year more than we take in as a nation--AND THIS DYNAMIC HAS CONTIN- UED FOR THE LAST TWENTY YEARS! So then, we need to tax the wealthy that are perceived to have more money than they could ever spend and who have made their wealth off the unjust abuse of the common person, and to overthrow the institutions that are perceived as inequitable.

THAT'S NOT THE SOLUTION!!!!!!! That movement is literally the demise of everything we have built in the last 244 years.

The angst we feel is valid, and the clear attempt to change the system is valid. However, the solution is not to centralize government programs and place MORE power in the hands of the oligarchy. This trajectory thrust us back into the Dark Ages where a king or ruling family owns the people.

Now about two thousand families own most of the wealth in the world. This ruling elite finance political campaigns, own the dominating corpora- tions, pay for the advertising that manipulates the masses and controls the media, endow the universities, and most of all, spread a plantation mentality that offers food, housing, and basic subsistence to the masses in return for a allegiance to their principles. The only difference between the dynamics of this time and the feudalism of the Dark Ages is that a small group of powerful people and organizations now own the people rather than a king.

We are at a critical crossroad. If we follow the road to excessive spending, debt, lack of accountability, and revolution, then we will fade into oblivion as these policies are not sustainable. The US economy will continue to weaken. We will lose our technical and military superiority. And the command economies of China and Russia, as well as the religious dictatorships of the world, will overtake our nation. It may be a gradual disintegration as the smaller democracies are likely to fall first, but that is the direction.

The only hope is the manifestation of the moral and political genius of our Founding Parents who built the most remarkable organization history has ever known with principles that have been PROVEN over the last 244 years.

If We the People manifest the intent of our Founding Charter, the power of ownership and decision-making will be given to each citizen: WE will govern, WE will determine how our tax dollars are spent, WE will assume the power that has been granted to us in the US Constitution and take the power back from the politicians, lobbyists, corporations, media, power brokers, the wealthy, the scientists, the academics, the technocrats, and all those that have subtly eroded or completely taken our rights to think, express ourselves, worship, protect ourselves and innovate, while minimizing the imposition of central dictates and while developing an educational system that prepares our children for a bright future.

We must not dismiss these factions as each one provides a critical part to our whole; however, we must NEVER forget that We the People reign supreme and are the Shareholders and the Decision-Makers in our Government.

We the People must elect officials who support Free Enterprise, develop healthy competition in the Marketplace, discover and finance businesses that counterbalance financial, cultural and systemic power-holds, provide resource independence, employ fiscal responsibility, minimize regulation, encourage privatization in all areas of government, and maintain our Human Rights, all as described heretofore.

Most immediately, we must elect officials that privatize our Social Security System. This one change will drastically change the social consciousness of our country. Owning a fund that each worker and their employer contributes to and accumulates at compound rates for an entire working life will infuse each person with a sense of hope in working in any position at any level, as the most menial of jobs will develop a fund of well over a million dollars over a worker's career.

People will become more committed to the U.S., a greater work ethic will develop, and a reduction in social services will occur as people become vested in the U.S. Legacies will be bequeathed, investments in property and communities will occur, and faith in the US way of life will be restored. These funds will necessarily have to be regulated just as IRA, 401Ks and SEP funds are regulated, but they will be owned by each worker. They should also be subject to loss if serious crimes or felonies are committed.

An excess of paternal values can lead to fascism and war. An excess of maternal values can lead to permissiveness and weakness. Excesses must be counterbalanced just as described earlier in relation to the economy. The authoritarian generally looks for approval of their efforts while the consensual looks for love and care. Respect for each group is critical for overall health as paternity offers strength and direction and maternity offers nurturing and inclusiveness, and both are necessary to the whole. This is not to say that any person or gender or group is entirely paternal or maternal, as all people, groups and institutions have a combination of values from each dichotomy. It is to say that dismissing, revolting against or disrespecting either side or either value destroys the integrity of the whole, while embracing conflicting positions makes us grow and develop. **We develop step-by-step, together, like climbing a spiral staircase.** We do not progress by revolting against earlier or opposing concepts. Respect and understanding allows for integration which guides progress. Violence only leads to eventual replication of the mistakes of the past.

CHAPTER XX.

The Proper Means of Change

First, change MUST be peaceful. Martin Luther King Jr.'s model for social change is the strongest and most effective in history. MLK relied upon the words in our Constitution to lead a non-violent movement that not only became ingrained in the consciousness of the people of the United States but also led to legislative changes that survive perpetuity. His monument in Washington, D.C. is a tribute to his remarkable impact, as are the name-sakes established in each community across the country. Non-violence makes a statement stronger than any destruction can muster and provides for growth that endures forever.

It is critically important that we implement changes in the United States, but the changes must be done properly. Our system provides a means for peaceful and civil change and we must make use of these means. If such means requires a non-violent stance, then so be it. The loud expression of silent, peaceful protest is more powerful than violence, destruction and looting, and more lasting. But "change" means doing what *you* can do to contribute in some way to make things better than the way you found things. It may mean getting involved with your community, your school system, your local, regional, or national governance. It may mean creating technology or hiring engineering or high tech firms to create technology that will solve problems.

It may mean supporting organizations that are leading the way to a better tomorrow that includes the responsible use of Human Rights and healthy implementation of Free Enterprise. Whatever it is, you as a US citizen are fortunate to have the opportunity to be here at this moment in history, and you are obligated to give back.

We MUST balance our US Budget and pay down our National Debt to no more than three times our National Income, if not to zero. That means passing a Balanced Budget Amendment, and stop spending an average of over $1 trillion dollars a year beyond our income. That means clarifying the various departments the U.S. funds each year via subcommittees. That means privatizing as many services as possible with government oversight, perfect accountability, and fiscal responsibility. That means using our resources better including the development of our children in our educational system.

We MUST assume our position as the Shareholders and the Decision-Makers in our Government as provided by our Constitution and our Founding Parents, and make our voices heard on how our tax dollars are spent and how we feel about every issue regarding our governance. That means creating a means for the taxpayers to determine how our tax dollars are spent, and removing this task from the lawmakers who have failed us and put us into debt so deep that it will require extraordinary changes to pay it off. That means voicing our positions on every major issue, every significant piece of proposed legislation, and every matter concerning our governance. That means moving from the recently developed oligarchical system in place now to the Democratic Republic our Founding Parents envisioned. That means counterbalancing all monopolistic centers of power: corporate, religious, racial, gender, sexual, and ideological. That means the government must study and determine such centers of power and offer financing to counterbalancing organizations, as healthy competition is the Market's natural means of regulation, while regulating only as necessary against abuses. That means using technology already available to create safe and accurate polling that offers secure communication so that We the People can tell our lawmakers what We the People want.

We MUST privatize the Social Security program for the sake of removing the burden from the US government, avoid additional taxation needed to maintain the program, and minimize the likely collapse of the Social Security Administration, while giving We the People the financial security we have invested in, we have been promised and we deserve! That means making all employees and the self-employed contribute to the Social Security System without earning caps, and using the additional funds to plan for the transition to privatization, while allowing workers newly contributing to the Social Security System to begin contributing to one's own private fund, similar to an IRA or 401K fund. This transition will take about fifty years without defaulting on obligations to those who paid into the system. It will increase the net worth of each worker in the U.S. It will create a "vesting" of the worker in the U.S., infusing a commitment to the country, increasing investment in one's property and in our communities, and reducing dependence on social programs, as each worker will amass well over $1 million dollars from compound growth during their work life. It will also offer a massive investment in the economy as financial institutions will lend on projects that will propel substantial and sustainable growth.

We MUST care for our planet as we are literally destroying the only home we have. Every day, we see the numerous signs of carbon emissions in our atmosphere causing the planet to warm, creating record breaking storms, massive wildfires, and unhealthy air quality. We have polluted our waterways, oceans and lands with debris and chemicals that have worked their way into our food supply and destroyed the pristine gifts of our beautiful blue planet. We are creating and storing hundreds of thousands of radioactive fuel rods that could literally cause the incineration of our planet.

In the last 150 years, we have increased our knowledge of ourselves, our planet and our universe to the point where we have made medical, scientific, and technological advances that have served to increase our life-spans over 100%. However, along with the advances we enjoy today have come significant new problems. It is the obligation of this and future generations to build upon the advances we have made and solve the problems that have presented themselves. Technology can increase communication, increase safe emissions of fossil fuels, create nuclear fusion, and clean up pollution.

These issues are not Right or Left issues, they are not Democratic or Republican issues, nor Green Party issues. These issues affect every US citizen and, by extension, everyone in the world. As we resolve the issues that this Democratic Republic is experiencing in its maturation, the entire world will benefit.

We are still the City on a Hill. We have challenges before us and mountains to climb, but as history has shown over the last fantastic 244 years, we will rise to the challenge and light the beacon into the future.

It will take time to make the transitions. Polling the people will take time to refine. It may take time for the people to adapt. The process may begin slowly. Patience is necessary as it takes a generation to incorporate any change into the consciousness of the people. But immediate committed movement in the right direction is absolutely necessary in order to bring about the change we want.

We are at a crossroad. One way continues down the road of massive, irresponsible overspending, maintaining a political body that does not serve the interests of the people, an oligarchy that has taken control of our lives, and a general lack of concern for the negative impact we have on each other and our planet. The other road follows more closely the genius of our Founding Parents to respect the inalienable rights of all individuals to think for ourselves, express ourselves, worship as we please, and protect ourselves and our families, while remaining free to innovate and problem-solve to improve our lives as we see fit, act fiscally responsible, determine how we want our tax dollars spent and voice our will for governing policies. The difference is clear. The correct road is clear. It's critical for us to take the correct road.

Despite our faults, together we have developed the most remarkable system that supports the sustenance, growth, and development of people the world has ever seen. WE MUST ACKNOWLEDGE THE GENIUS OF OUR FOUNDING PARENTS AND THEIR VISION FOR A DEMOCRATIC REPUBLIC BUILT ON HUMAN RIGHTS AND EMPLOYING FREE ENTERPRISE. WE MUST APPRECIATE THE ACCOMPLISHMENTS THAT WE'VE MADE IN 244 YEARS THAT ARE UNRIVALLED IN THE HISTORY OF CIVILIZATION WHILE STILL CARING FOR

OUR VULNERABLE. AND WE MUST BUILD UPON WHERE WE ARE NOW BY MORE CLOSELY MANIFESTING THE PRINCIPLES IN OUR FOUNDING CHARTER OF THESE UNITED STATES, NEVER DIMINSHING THEIR VALUE, REVOLTING AGAINST THEM OR DESTROYING THEM.

This generation has inherited a gift like no other generation in history as a citizen of the United States of America, and a person living on this beautiful earth in the twenty-first century. Now it is your responsibility to recognize what you have and take it to the next level as you fix the inevitable problems of progress and growth.

Dear Reader,

You have just read THE MOST IMPORTANT MESSAGE of our time. If you found this book or any part of this book interesting, you may get much more information at our website: www.MarkABuzzotta.com.

You may place orders at this site. You may obtain video presentations of much of the material. You may explore additional books written by this author. And you may communicate with us.

We encourage your feedback, thoughts and ideas as our intent to is to perfect our system of government and the social organizations that we share. We believe that this endeavor is a cooperative and developing process, so your contribution is valued. Please write us at LetsMakeStraightOurWay@gmail.com. We will not publish your email address or any other contact information, but we may use all or part of the content of your correspondence in future published products and presentations, so if you would like any limitations on using the information you send us, please indicate so in your correspondence.

Thank you for engaging your thoughtful consideration in THE MOST IMPORTANT issues of our time.

Sincerely,
Mark A Buzzotta